OUR FAMILY

The young daughters of Lin Yutang, the Chinese author, are following in his footsteps. Pieces of theirs written in Chinese have already begun to appear in magazines in their native land. Their English writing, begun as exercises in the language, developed into diaries and from that, with a little prompting from their father, into comments and descriptions on places they visit, people they see, and especially on their own family life and their memories of China.

From these writings have been selected—but *not* revised or edited—the contents of this book. It is offered not as a curiosity, not as a juvenile, but as the fresh and keen observation of young minds. Adet at 16, Anor at 13 and Mei-mei at 8, have seen America and France, with glimpses too of Italy and England. They remember China fondly and with a patriotism heightened by the Japanese invasion.

Perhaps best of all, they know their famous father through and through and can write about him and their mother with affectionate candor and humor. In these pages the reader becomes intimate with one of the most delightful and original families ever enclosed within book covers — a Chinese father and mother and their three daughters.

Photograph by Carl Van Veck

ADET, ANOR AND MEIMEI

OUR FAMILY

BY ADET AND ANOR LIN

with a foreword and comments
by MEIMEI

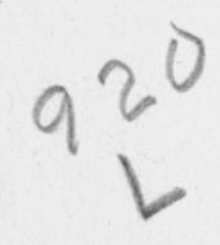

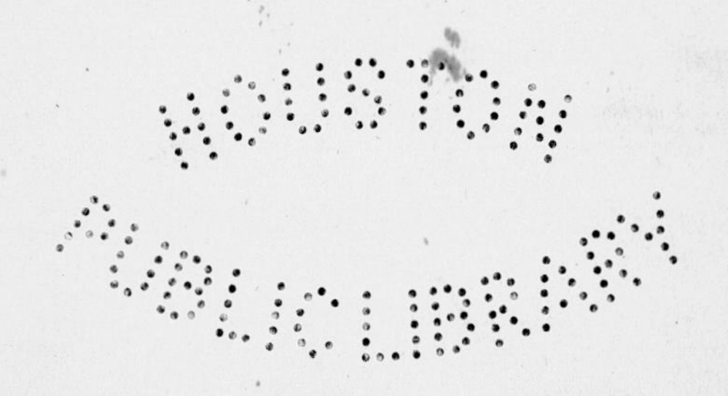

THE JOHN DAY COMPANY
New York

MANUFACTURED IN THE UNITED STATES OF AMERICA

Van Rees Press · New York

To Our Parents

Introduction

THERE is no particular reason why anyone should introduce these children, Adet, Anor and Meimei Lin, to those who will read and enjoy this book. In the first place, everybody knows their famous father, Lin Yutang, and those who know him personally know, too, the children's equally delightful mother. I introduce the children, therefore, purely for my own pleasure, because I have enjoyed them so much as they have been in my home, have romped with my children, have talked and laughed and acted in little plays with them—in short, while they were behaving in all those fresh, spontaneous ways proper to their age and intelligence. And I have enjoyed all this the more because never once have I seen them forget the beautiful courtesy natural to Chinese family life. Somehow within this exquisite shape of courtesy in human relationships Chinese children still act and speak with the freedom of imagination and instinct.

These little essays which Adet and Anor have written, and Meimei's comments, are simply further expressions of this happy combination. They were begun at the suggestion of their father and without intent of publication. But they soon went beyond any suggestions. The children found it fun to write and we found it fun to read. It is all entirely their own writing. No adult has changed or corrected. When the children heard their manuscripts were to be published, they re-read them and themselves made such small changes as they wished. This surely is the privilege of any author.

The reader will soon see that each child writes in her own individual way. And indeed, they are very different, Adet, Anor and Meimei.

Adet is the most Chinese, and at least at her present age the most subjective and idealistic. She never forgets for one moment that she is Chinese. She has the slender beauty the Chinese most admire, the gentle voice and thoughtful look. All her contact with the western world only seems to make her more exquisitely Chinese.

Anor is not so much Chinese as herself. A very sturdy personality proclaims itself from what she writes, as it does from her real presence. One feels it, intelligent, incisive and not afraid of its own difference. Anor will always be a little different whether she is in China or abroad. But she is strong enough to bear it. I should not be surprised one day to see an actual genius declare itself in those clear eyes of hers. I sometimes think I see it now.

As for Meimei—what is she? A kitten, a doll, a sedate small lady—whatever she is, she is clever enough to keep us all wondering and expecting from one moment to the next.

Here, then, is the world as it appears to these little Chinese girls, whose eyes look out upon it freshly and unspoiled. But we see through them more than the outer world. We see also into a charming, simple family life, an expression at its modern best of the old Chinese family which has stood for centuries as the basis of the world's most lasting civilization.

PEARL S. BUCK

Foreword

by Meimei

FATHER told Adet and Anor to write some diary. Soon they began to write and it became very good, so Father told them that maybe it can be published. When we came to Paris, they continued to write more and more. Some times we have someone read them, they are very interesting and real. Especially Anor's. I like "Rats and Mice" the best. Do you? Every morning Anor sits in her room and writes something, the moment she hears a new word like "As Pat as Butter" tomorrow she will put it in the diary. About Adet I don't know much. I will tell you some more about Anor. Anor forbade us to read the Morning of July 14th. I think there must be something in it. I don't see why Because if she forbided us to read why she won't be scared to let the others to read it. When some-one reads a new word, she will hide her face toward the sofa. Adet writes less because she is writing Chinese. Adet is 16 years old and Anor is 13. Good-bye!

Contents

Part II. AMERICA

Part III. EUROPE

Part IV. CHINA

Part I. THE FIVE LINS

Why Am I Me?

By Anor

SOMETIMES I think why I am born in a human being, and why I am named Anor Lin, and why I am Lin Yutang's daughter.

I often wondered why I am not born a dog or a cat or an elephant. Suppose I were an elephant, what would I do? Should I live in the woods, or be locked in one of the cages in the Central Park Zoo? If I were a horse, what kind of suroundings I have?

I think of such things often. But no one can answer me. Suppose I were a tree and people cut one of my branches off, would I feel it or would I be glad to have it off? If I am one of the whales in the big oceans, and people catch me what would I feel and what it is like to be a whale?

Now what I am born in a Chinese fimaly, why am I not a German, or French, or an Englishman or American? More over why I am not one of the savages in the time of Columbus?

Then who made me a girl? I like to be a boy. Who is the one who decides that I should be a girl. Does he know that I like to be a boy? Then who says that I should be born in 1926 and at April First?

Then who says that I should have ten fingers and two eyes and one mouth etc. Such things that no one can prove how it is done. Now since I am me why am I me?

THE LIN'S BANNER

Father

By Anor

I WAS told to write a scatch of my parents and sisters, and here it is. I am going to start with father.

My father, the forty-four-year old man who always gets mix up when he comes to the age problem. He counts the Chinese age for himself. But when he comes to our age it is just a mass. For instance we count both Chinese and American ages, and increase one on new year and one on our birthdays, which means we add two in one year. So he finally had proudly decided that we will all be Chinese and count the new year as our birthdays in spite of the birthday cakes in April, May, July, August and October.

Father always says that his feet are the cleanest in the world, because every time he comes home from a walk he always washes his feet, and says, "Mine are the cleanest in the world! Who's are cleaner then mine? President Roosevelt? Hitler? Mussolini? Nobody can compare with mine. I don't think they wash them thrice or four times a day like me." That's the joke he often says.

Father is very fond of *roast beef* and it is getting

more and more well-known about it. Every time we go to Mr. R.W.'s home, we are bound to have roast beef.

Father loves to go to little shops and look around but he saves money by not buying them every time.

Father hates lectures and little articles, but in spite he writes them just the same in New York because they are good.

Lin Yutang writes wonderful books and read and re-read them for at least six times. He is very fond of travelling and go to places where it is worth going. Like Paris, London, Peking places where he can write a best-seller book. But in spite of that he wrote an American best seller in New York. The place where he calls "hell".

Father is the favorite son of grandfather's and is the most successful among his brothers. He often tells us about his youth. Sometime it makes mother chuckle. Also he often talks about the future when he will have a moustache and beard. He likes very much to feel mother's cheek and does it every day. Father claims that he is the twin with Meimei.

Father is very fond of taking a bath as his exersise. The only sport he takes is walking. But in his youth he was the *winner of the one mile runners in the St. John's University*. Father plays the piano well but can't get one single piece memerized.

He likes the country and mountains. When he has a mountain to look at he often watches it and admires it. Father hates the sticky skyscrapers. "It is because" he says, "they don't have a frontage."

Father dislikes young men who comb their hair very neat and put a quarter of a bottle of hair cream on.

He likes brown, heavy, water-proof, well polished, wearable, warm, swell shoes.

Father always laughs at the jokes which he told for many times, but every time he says there is something to laugh at and nobody gets tired of them.

Father loves changings like going out to dinner with the family but not in a formal dress because he hates to dress like a waiter.

Father too wants beauty. He changed his framed glasses into the new kind without any frame. He knows how to match his suit, shirt with his necktie.

Father has a marverlas degestion. Once he wrote to mother and said, "My stomack can digest every thing but rubber." That made us laugh. Also it is true. I never heard of father being indigest in his stomack. At night if he gets hungry he gets up and fry eggs or eat any thing he likes. When he is sick he eats just as much, or maybe more. He says that's how he gets well. When mother is ill he wonders why doesn't she eat or drink as usual?

[*Papa often koi with me at lunch time. Koi is the sound when we put our necks together.—Meimei*]

Mother

By Anor

MOTHER weighs about 113 pounds. I think that is not much. But mother mentions the word "FAT" almost 8 times per day. When her friend says to her she is thiner, Mother doesn't believe it, but says "nonsense". Mother diets once a week. In the restaurant when you have good food mother forgets all about dieting but eats as much as she likes. I consider it good and we all hope she will do that every day. But she doesn't. Sometimes she gets sick out of it.

Mother also knows how to play the piano. The tunes she plays often are home songs.

Mother loves to discuss family incidents and also our fortune. The thing she likes is to let father sit in a chair and not reading anything but smoking if he likes to and hear her talking without any moving or uttering a sound.

Mother sometimes is very happy and does many things unusual to please us. Like playing games with us and sitting on the swing, etc. When mother is angry she and her anger are very quiet all day. Neither of them talked to each other till both of them had almost busted then anger speaks.

Father always says that mother is a warm hearted woman and it is true. Mother likes company very much, and she likes to talk about things but never gets tied till she stops. Then mother won't feel well.

Mother likes order and regularity. She went to office every day in New York when the war broke out. Mother and her friend talked and laughed in the office. But they worked too.

Mother is very good to servants and every servant likes her as they serve her.

Mother is a fish-eater. No matter how bad the fish is she eats them just the same. Sometimes she eats a fish alone, when we don't want it. The servants that had worked with mother all know that mother likes FISH. I do see why mother doesn't get tired of fish, because there are so many kinds. But to father's ROAST BEEF it is just one kind, but he doesn't get tired of it.

Why mother is so popular is that she follows every thing father does. Such as going to hear father's lectures, and so forth.

When father is writing books mother always says, "Don't write too long, Y.T. People won't like to read it." Then every time what she said was wrong she would say, "Larp sarp kong" for many days till she laughed at herself.

Mother often talks with her hand. She does it in a funny way. Often it makes us laugh. Sometimes when she is working she cross her fingers for no reason. People say that mother's hands look good luck. Some say that she will have a long life. Some say that everything that past through her hands will turn good. Thus mother is very proud of her hands. Also she is proud of her nose. It is very rare to see a Chinese nose so pointed and straight as hers. When mother doesn't laugh the only way is to tell father to talk about her nose, then she would naturely smile.

Mother is very afraid of people saying she is fat. In her youth time when she was going to marry father, Grandfather said to the sedan chair carriers that the sedan chair had got to be a bigger one because the bride was fat. Grandfather didn't mean it seriously. But mother's sister heard it and told mother. Mother was so mad at herself that a few days before the wedding mother took a kind of medicine that would make her thin. Now that mother is thiner then before father admits that mother was fat when she was a bride.

[*Mother is a nice person. She likes every one. She is so warm and soft.—Meimei*]

Adet

By Anor

ADET is the eldest sister in our family. First I want to describe how she looks.

Father says that she has Chinese beauty in her face. Adet's eyes are bright. She has a round face and dark eyebrows.

Adet is a clever girl. She helps mother from time to time. She writes very well and reads very fast. Sometimes she cares for others too much that the way she acts often makes us laugh.

Adet is very stylish. She knows all the time what kind of hair to wear for what season. She combs her hair for five or six times per day. When she is reading, sometimes she would get up in the middle of the period and comb her hair. As to her dresses, to be sure, she knows what should go with what, and what color matches with her shoes, coats, etc. She knew exactly what fashion was going on in America when she was in New York for what season. I think that's enough for her liking of dresses.

Adet Lin reads a lot of books. A thick book would last her for only one or two days, but now I read almost as quick.

She also likes to dress Meimei as her doll; and put pins and things on her dresses. She knows what side should she wear a hat. Things like that which she is the only one in the family who knows. In spite of all that I've said she is still a good girl. She tries very hard to help her sisters. She has patience which is she can wait for a long time for certain things.

Mother and Father always say that she is a grown up. But she still plays hide and seek with her sisters but not very often about twice a year. Adet also cooks oranges with us in the garden.

Adet likes to arrange flowers. Her taste is good and the arrangements are not bad at all.

Adet often laughs at some things which we don't see any thing to laugh at, but she does.

Adet falls on the floor very often. She always breaks very valuable things like Mother's glasses, a big flower pot, sometimes a bowl of soup. Adet doesn't walk very nicely. She doesn't look at the road when she walks. Her feet are very long and thin. They are not very strong. When she falls, she does not do any thing to it but sits just on the floor and laughs for at least five minutes.

Adet's favorite movie stars are Loretta Young, Katherine Hepburn, Louise Rainer and Ronald Colman. She doesn't permit me to say so but it is true. She says, "It is not true, and Anor is cheating me. Don't believe it if she says it is true because I have no favorites." I personally don't think there is any harm. But she thinks so. Believe me that it is true, because she said so in Florence. I am sure she likes Shirley Temple better than Menjou. So that proofs that she surely has some favorites. Poor Adet, she is angry at me now because I said so.

Adet often goes out with her friends. She is very polite with them and is also mouse-like. But at home she does any thing she likes to, even scolding her sisters, but not often.

Adet has her goodness and badness. The average mark for her is 88. She is a good sister to us. The mark for it is about 93. I hope she will be satisfied with the marks I gave her.

Meimei

By Anor

MEIMEI is seven and half years old. She had a picture taken in Italy which looks like, father says, "Twenty-nine years old." It was our great suprise to hear that. But sometimes she acts just like thirty. She does everything neatly and nicely. But it takes her an hour to dress sometimes.

Meimei sometimes wants to be patted and says baby language like, "I know only two word," "I am one month old." Sometimes it is cute, but sometimes it makes me mad as a tiger.

Meimei often is very naughty and bad. For instance, she won't listen to anything I say. To get my parent's encouragement she would do it nicely and feels that she is a good girl. I hate that sort of things. She is very proud of her stamp colection because people always say, "Oh, how clever you are. You do it so well." Everybody has to say it because she is small.

It's true that she does it well. But sometimes her proudness is too strong that she won't even let me touch or look at her stamp album.

Meimei does other things very nicely and quietly. As to her quietness, for instance, the most she says in a meal is three or four sentences.

Meimei's writing and drawing are very nice. The

things she draws every time in her pictures are houses and a red sun. Her writings are neat sometimes better than mine. Her writings are like this

abcdefghi etc

Meimei likes to fill black the letters like this

She does it on the books and people's writings. She picks something out of the waste-paper-basket, and fills the letters black.

Meimei likes to imitate funny people and says who looks like who. One of Meimei's toes looks like a certain old woman. She is a fat woman and so is Meimei's toe.

When her sisters tease her she would get very angry and stick her lower lip out for some time and say "Wăy' stăr pĭt," it means "Will you stop it!" But she uses her bad English to show that she is angry.

Meimei has four dolls, three big ones and two small ones. She loves the smallest one because it is small. Meimei always puts water in him. Meimei has tried very hard to make socks for him. But it wasn't a success every time.

Meimei is intelligent. She knows what the grown-ups are talking and knows what it means. She often takes a big breathe in the middle of her talking. Meimei has a stone collection. She picks any stone from the beach or the garden and puts it in her collection. She says they are as precious as dimons.

When Meimei is reading or studying her morning lessons she would pull a chair to a place where she gets sunshine. After doing that she would slowly write her new words down.

Meimei learns things quickly. She knows how to spell "Conversation" and "Mussolini" etc. Words like that which I didn't know how to spell until this year.

Meimei depents on mother very much. At night she always sits in the same chair with mother and holds mother tightly with her little hands.

When Meimei is doing arithmetic she would say the tables all out for instance 32 devided by 8 is how much, how much, how much? 3 times, no. 4 times,—yes." That is why it takes her so long to do things.

Meimei plays the piano well. She wants people to teach her. If it is too hard for her she would say the teacher is no good.

Meimei has made a good friend with someone who she has never talked with. That is the French electrition [at Menton]. She remembers him and mentions him almost everyday.

Meimei these days often says "What do you mean" when people talk to her. A very simple thing would make her ask.

Meimei

By Adet

I WAS asked to do a description of each of the five members of the family. Anor has begun with the eldest, and I shall begin with the youngest: Meimei.

Meimei is a very small and intelligent girl. She is supposed to be 8 years old, but still looks as if just

4 or 5. Often she acts just like a grown-up and talks very decently and asks questions like these: "Isn't Russia wanting to let the Russian women have many children like Germany?" "Is France for China or Japan?" If she keeps on like that, I think she will grow up to be a politician. Questions like "How do they build bridges?" "How does the locomotive move?" often make me so helpless. Often I change to another subject or say it is very hard to explain. Meimei is also very understanding, sometimes when her parents or sisters tell her not to do that for such and such reasons, she would quietly obey. But sometimes when she understands what it means and still like to do it, her face would turn to a half laughing half angry face and says, "Why?" and after the reason is explained, she would say, "Why?" and on and on until I stop talking.

When she is naughty, she is quite naughty and says naughty and scolding sentences. She knows quite well how to answer back when her sisters quarrel with her.

She is very often the messager and delivery girl of the family. When she is willing she does not mind errands, but if you tell her to do too much, she would scornfully refuse no matter how you praise her.

She plays the piano fairly well and reads pretty quickly. Her sewing, knitting and card skills are often surprising.

Meimei has a funny habit and that is to put her hands under mother's arms. Whenever she is sitting with mother she would tuck her hands under mother's arms. Often a time she puts her own hands under her own arms. Just now I can hear her angry and stamping on the floor at Anor's teasing. Meimei is shy and bashful when she is with strangers. She never talked English when one of us was present, but now she is beginning to speak it. Because she is the youngest she often gets special privileges and she enjoys them.

She is very slow at her morning toilette and yet puts away her slippers and pajamas very neatly. She likes decorations on her dress; pins and clips. Almost every time I have to choose a dress for her to wear before she sleeps. She can not decide it for herself and she listens to my judgment. If I choose a pretty dress and mother allows she would be very happy and says, "Weeee! Good! Good!" and sleeps very nicely. She is afraid of mouse and darkness, often before going into a room she would drag me to turn on the light for her and then she would do other things by herself. Julia (one of our cousins) and she look very much alike when they smile and they declared themselves as twins. When she is with Julia she would turn against Anor and me and say: "We, whose faces are alike."

Meimei sometimes pretends and acts to be very babish. She likes to be treated as a baby and seems not to understand anything and then after the explanation she laughs at herself as a grown up. She is usually very ambitious at learning new things, new games and new words, and she learned them very quickly. She loves to play anagrams, but she seldom plays it. Mother is always her partner and what Meimei does is to draw the checkers and be the telephone of the parents about words. But she always enjoys sitting beside mother and laughs at funny things that happen.

She has a very elderly hobby and it is *STAMPS*

COLLECTION. Last Summer father bought a stamp book for the family to play away the leisure time. We did not take great interest in it but Meimei did and gradually it has become her book and her hobby. Now she has about over one thousand stamps. The funny thing is that she can distinguish Rumania's stamps from Belgium's. I think she knows more names of the countries than I do now. Since then father taught her many stamps and she is always greatly pleased. Night before last we received a letter from Russian by Yu Ming, and there were three aviation stamps on it. Meimei was terribly pleased and was extremely cheerful all along the dinner which she seldom talks much.

Meimei has many dolls. The prettiest and biggest is Barbara that we won from the shops in Atlantic City, and her favorite is "Rubber". Mother gave it to her at Xmas in 1935 and it is because mother gave it to her and of its flexibility and cuteness that it has become Meimei's favorite. It is made of rubber and its head can be taken off. Meimei often baths him and takes its head off to pour the water out. It's name has come from its material—rubber. Meimei often plays with her dolls alone, changes different dresses for them and washes their dirty clothes. She loves to play with water and even in winter; sometimes when she has nothing to do she would wash dirty handkerchieves for pleasure, but not too dirty ones. She loves Lux's soap flakes and shakes them into thousand bubbles.

[*Now I have 8 big dolls and 3 small. I have two Mexican which Julia gave us. Rubber has a big stomach.—Meimei*]

Anor

By Adet

ANOR is a cute girl and she is very American-like ever since she was a little girl in China—straight forward, less-quiet and lively. She is now over twelve months; sometimes she acts like thirteen and sometimes ten. When she is very good she is very good and when she is very naughty she is indeed naughty. She is often very keen on doing things, if we have a new game, she would want to do it almost twice or thrice a day. If I played that game with her for 5 times continuously she would still say let us play once more.

She is often the most adventurous of the three. Such as climbing high trees and touching frightful worms, but she is darned scared of cats. You ought to see her facial expression when she meets a cat scared as a mouse. The reason she is so scared of it is that she once saw a group of newly born kittens and since that minute she has become so afraid of cats.

Anor is very timid among her classmates whenever one of us is present, but I don't know about other times; I think she is just as timid. Twice she invited her American schoolmates and before her guests arrived she begged me to lead all the games and talk a lot with them. I said that it was her party but she insisted on me being the hostess. I do not like it. Often she said, "Let's play a game." The guests would say: "What game?" Then she would look at me and talk to me in Chinese to tell me to explain. I said she must explain, but she would just say nothing and looked at me while the guests paused quietly for one minute or so; then I was forced to speak.

Sometimes when she came back from school she told on the classmate that teased or did something to her and filled herself with anger. Mother would say, "Why didn't you answer back?" Anor didn't, and said nothing and sometimes put the anger on Meimei and me.

Anor is often very gay and wants to tease me or Meimei on one particular sentence that was said wrong. At the beginning of her teasing she always has the victory and then if I don't answer back, her teasing would be in vain. Then I would tease back just one sentence and often then she would change the teasing into anger and stop talking for the whole half hour.

She loves to play the piano and her fingers are very powerful. She learns and memorizes very quickly. She has now about 7 or 8 tunes that she memorizes very thoroughly. The tunes she plays are generally marches and 4/4 times. She doesn't like melodies and minuets but recently she is beginning to play "Melody in F".

Anor loves to be a teacher. Since she was very small she likes to teach Meimei Arithmatic. She is usually a good instructor but sometimes when Meimei does not know her work and can not answer quickly, she would shout at her and tell her to take the book back. Anor herself is a studious girl. She often prepares her lesson till late; father often tells her to stop preparing her lessons, but she continues. She loves to go to movies and plays, when father or mother suggests we might go to see a movie she would show her great pleasure on her face. Whenever she is allowed to see a movie she always welcomes.

Anor invents very funny words and names. Some are very cute and some are awful and mother dislikes those. Some of them have become so common that every one of the five uses them. Chinese and American visitors never can understand them unless explained. They are often very convenient.

I like to see her doing outdoor exercises. She is always wonderful at things. Her most charming expression is when she is gay, lively and a bit naughty. Her jokes often cheer up the family. She has picked up English idioms and phrases very quickly and she uses them at the very right time.

Mother

By Adet

MOTHER is a wonderful woman and is always very much admired and loved by her family and friends. She treats the maids and servants very kindly and talks to them very much which father never does. When giving tips she would say days before not to be too lenient about or otherwise they will be spoiled, but when the day has come mother would ask me to take her hand bag and give the maid about 150% of the said amount. That shows her kindness.

When friends come to dinner at our home or the restaurant, mother serves her guest very well and looks after their plates to see that they are not empty. Often she herself doesn't have enough. When a guest steps in and obliged to stay for dinner, mother always prepares a very decent meal and sometimes too much to be finished. The guest always enjoys and mother is satisfied with the guest appetite while she herself is hungry. That shows her sincerety.

Mother is very honest. Often father lies that his purse was lost or something like that. She often believes sincerely and then father laughs out. She would say: "Naughty boy trying to fool me." That shows her honesty.

She often works very hard herself to help the maid in cooking and washing. She does work which she can have a maid do for her, but she does it herself willingly. Mother brushes all the overcoats herself instead of sending them to the presser. Father appreciates her on this manner very much.

Yet, when we are to enjoy ourselves, mother doesn't mind paying a little more to get the real joy. She enjoys greatly after a good picture or dinner.

Mother always takes the safe side either in food or the care of her children. She rather stays in the house with the children than go out with father when the children will be left with a maid. She says if she goes with father and thinks about her children all the time she wouldn't enjoy the trip at all. We appreciate her on this very much.

Once when we visited Wusih without Meimei for the weekend when Meimei was about 4, Mother could not take her mind off though Meimei was perfectly safe with her nurse Wangma. Then we didn't stay for the night but hurried home by night train. She was extremely glad to have Meimei in her arms.

Mother likes to talk over things very much with father or us or her nieces. She enjoys it but often after talking too much and getting excited she would feel a headache. The family always enjoys her stories of her girlhood, and how they enjoy the new year eves.

Mother does not have a habit of smoking but she always welcomes a cigarette or two after dinner. She is left handed in cutting or doing heavier work, yet when we take the needles in our left hands she would have us change them immediately. Her handwriting is neat and clear, unlike many people who just scrap down words and run along very fast.

Mother is often very quick-tempered and her voice spreads quite far when she talks loudly. When some one treats or talks to her very impudently mother can never find a word to answer back. Afterwards she would be very angry and always regrets that she hadn't answered back. But then meeting the impudent person again she would treat him or her just as nicely as an usual guest. We always tell mother to be crueler than usual but she can not do it. Mother often reminds father of little things such as haircut, baths, etc. Father does not like them especially a haircut. He often takes a haircut for mother's sake. Mother also treats father like her elder son; she would pour lots of milk in father's cup quietly and wants father to drink it without any notice. Father often discovers and either pours the milk back or drinks it as mother wishes.

We three children and father always do funny and childish things and mother is always the elderly person in the house; tells us to be careful with the carpet or the tables.

Once in a while mother would be very playful and agrees to do anything we wish.

Mother loves to buy shoes and she enfarsizes on stockings and shoes. She said, "Feet is the foundation of beauty." When we live in New York mother does not buy much besides shoes and stockings for she had her dresses made in China. Walking along 57th Street there are plenty of shoe shops. She can stand looking at the shoes for such a long time. She has small but rather beautiful feet; her legs are pretty. She has quite a lot of shoes all very nice-looking.

[*Mamma loves her pointed nose and is proud of it.—Meimei*]

Father

By Adet

FATHER is a very interesting person. He is always very natural with himself wherever he goes. He is always at home with anybody.

When father is working he is very serious; he has a study and when he works he always shuts the doors up; of course it is very natural with an author. Father seldom reads a novel and it is very funny. He usually reads essays, books of philosophy and of science. When he reads a novel he always reads it for a certain reason. Now he is reading more novels because he is writing a novel himself. When father reads a witty sentence he shows a delight on his face and if he comes upon a funny part he would laugh out so loud which I can never do. Father is the children's leader when he is leisure. Father starts games and invents them for us and often plays with us as an elder brother. He likes to talk of funny things and he likes to tease mother.

Father drinks tea and smokes quite a great deal. He says that he is sorry to miss the joy of drinking wine for he does not know what fun it is to drink that juice. In the morning he always has a tea pot and cup on his desk. He always drinks the tea and enjoys his pipe before he starts his work.

Father likes to travel a lot. He likes to see new places and discover something in it. The best is that he can enjoy both Chinese and foreign amusements, both city and country joys. He always enjoys a good movie and also a sleep under the pine trees. Father always tells us about Peking where city and country combine. Father hates Shanghai for it does not have hills or outing places, but he stayed there for ten years.

Father takes great interest in our education. Sometimes during a walk he will tell us about "mankind" or "detraction of light," and in teaching he always has great patience.

Father loves mother a great deal and so is mother to father. Sometimes on a lecture tour father had to go to Detroy or Chicago for three days. They always miss each other a great deal—of course so do we.

When father writes he always writes in the way he talks. He uses simple, good, clear English. He often just dictates an article to the secretary in the morning. Father has several Chinese friends whom he values a great deal. These people are scholars. Father and his friends would go on a trip in seeking the grave of an ancient brilliant lady or visiting certain poet's old residents.

When Father Writes

By Anor

ACCORDING to my standard father is a real author, or maybe I am just boasting. When father writes it seems that the whole kingdom of the house is his and no one dares to disturb him but the peddlars in the streets. It is really a sight to see him write. When you enter his study it is just a simple but cozy one, with book shelves all around and in a very private corner stands the working desk—always so neat. He usually has his doors shut when he works and as I said, no one dares to disturb father. And when he gets through you can see smoke as clouds floating on the air and a smell of the pipe. Then you could see in the middle of the desk stands a pile of paper and beside it the manuscrips that he had worked that day. On the desk are just a few of his favorite books and some pens, pencils and a magnifying glass which he loves. The ash tray is usually filled and under his desk are still some ashes and some matches.

Mother some times dares to open his door and go in for something very nesseccary but when the door is opened we just dare to peek from the holes and father never looks up who is coming when he writes, but he knows.

Most of his articles are already planed out in his bed when it is really quiet, and Mother only dares to make a little noise when she turns over the pages in her book. There is another style when he thinks in bed. That is when all the lights in the house are out, and he would get up and go to the window and look at the view from the window, and the only thing one can see is a red light which is in the pipe. There he sits, so quiet and peaceful till every thing is planed out, but this does not happen often.

Some times you can see father smiling as he writes and that is as he tells us, the sign of good writing for, Father says, when one writes with a gloomy face the thing is sure to be bad, since the writer hates it himself how can the reader possibly be interested in it?

When Father has a secertary it is another way different. The girl sits on a chair and while father, with two hands in the pocket, walks around and dictates his lines, the only thing you could hear from another room is the rhithem of the type-writer. Father would sometimes put his feet on the window-shelf or on any place while he sits, for, he says, it would look ridiculous when he sits like a student, and at the same time it is uncomfortible.

So that's how father writes a book!

Mother Insists on Useing Toothpaste

By Anor

Mother likes cleaness and rules. Father doesn't care but does what he thinks is right.

One day as I was going to bed, mother said,

"Anor, be sure to use your toothpaste. Keep your teeth clean!" There the despute begins. Father said, "No, Anor, toothpaste is no use. Just take a cup of water and wash your mouth with it. That is enough. Don't use your tooth brush."

"No, Y.T.," said Mother, "You must let the child use both toothpaste and toothbrush. Anor, don't listen to your Father's talking. Now go." "Hong, don't you know that the scientists have proved that one *doesn't* have to use toothpaste? All you do is eat the right things" said Father reflectively. But mother says that she knows and told me at least to use salt. Father laughed and said, "I am going to the dentist to-morrow and let him examine my teeth. Then for five years I won't touch a toothbrush but wash my mouth with water *only*. Then I will go to the same dentist and see if I get any worse." Mother was helpless then. But said, "Look at your teeth now. See how you smoke. That your teeth are all black." Father said that he lets the dentist clean every year. Mother shut the arguement and said, "Anor, it is late, go and brush your teeth with toothpaste and brush. Good night." So I went to bed just as mother ordered and Father was disappointed. But didn't go to the doctor the next day.

Father's Hobbies

By Anor

IN certain times I think Father is just like us, a child. He has many hobbies, such as, playing with candles, coloring our books with many colors, and many others. About the usual hobbies men have he has them also.

First, to be sure, smoking. Father smokes almost all the time he wakes, even in bed. Father has to smoke when he writes. He says if he doesn't, he won't get anything out if he doesn't smoke. Once Father forgot his pipe, and he says that his hands felt empty and lazy, because he had nothing to hold. When Father goes in a deparment store, and they won't allow him to smoke, Father would say that he will never step into the store again.

Second, Father's tea. He also says that he needs his tea every morning. So that he can write. Sometimes when the tea is not hot enough, Father would drink one mouthful and then says, "Oh, dishwater, half hot and half cold. Take it away!" Father insists on useing a seperate pot for boiling the water. If the tea has a beef tea smell in it, it certainly would taste no good. Father would immediately demand another pot for boiling water for the tea.

Another hobby Father has is walking. He walks unsualy fast. When the family goes out Father is always walking ahead. Mother walks slow. So, Father always walks with me. Mother walks with Adet. Meimei is always with Mother. When Mother wears her mink coat, Father would want to walk together with her. "Because," Father says "people would look down upon me if I don't walk with you. And if I do, they would say, 'his wife has a mink coat, so he must be pretty well off!'" So there is a rule that if mother wears her mink coat, Father is supposed to walk with her.

As to the things Father plays with us, there are many. One is dripping candles. We make faces, horses, houses, and many things. It is fun. Father buys candles of many colors and we make many things out of them. Once when Mother was in the hospital, Father made a wax picture of her. It looked like her. We soon began to make boxes. The colors were so nice that we used one of them for putting stamps.

Father has so many other hobbies that I can't write them all down.

Father's Hobbies

By Adet

FATHER has quite a few hobbies. They are all very interesting. The first one is wax dripping.

On a painted home boat in Soochow we were enjoying ourselves with different self-made games. We had several candles on the little oak table. Father atempted to drip the candle on the table into a duck. The duck was made but it was very preliminary. We were enormously enthusiastic about it. When we returned to Shanghai after the weekend, we bought different colored candles. We dripped a color on a piece of glass so that it would be smooth when we cut it out, and when the wax was about just soft enough to cut and hard enough to stay we used a sharp knife and cut it into a form of house or tree or face. And when that piece was dry we dripped again a different color at the sides of a house or etc. and cut it in the same manner. When the picture was made, we used the flat of the knife and lifted the picture up. We were awfully glad to discover this new art craft. It also takes a skill to do it. Father always enjoys doing it and he is extremely proud to show it to his friends. One of the friends also tried on it and she did much better than we did. When we came to New York we still continued this pleasure of making pictures with wax. But we always hate to clean up, because when candle wax sticks to the table it is always so hard to pick it up.

Father has the hobby of collecting gramaphone records. He loves good music and likes to hear it over and over again. He has about 180 pieces. After dinner he would enjoy some good music before the fireplace, with the lights all out, except the flames of the log fire.

Father rather likes a walk in the country. On a clear morning with its fresh air perhaps, or with well-protected rubbers walking in an awaking rain, or wandering or sowntering in the woods with his pipe.

Father Eats at Midnight

By Anor

FATHER is very good at eating in the midnight. Mother laughs at him very often.

Once he felt hungry and fried 5 eggs and ate two pieces of crakers. Another time he ate 4 biscuits, and many other times too.

FATHER EATS AT MIDNIGHT

Father said, "I felt so hungray last night and I thought about ten minutes whether I should get up or not, but I felt ashamed of my self if I ate, but if I don't I can't go to sleep." So he got up and ate the things in the dining room. Mother chuckled and told us all about it.

"Poor me, I felt a little better, but still a little hungry," Father said. Mother is always so glad to see him eat. But laughs at him also. Often I wake up in the morning and find oranges, pears, etc. on the table near father.

Some times you would hear a noise from the kitchen in the night. You can almost be sure to know who it is.

Hunger is the worse thing I think about Father. He hates people having dinner at 8:00 or later. When he is invited at 8:00 he would eat with us first and then go.

One thing I like about being a father is that he can eat fried eggs anytime and it alway smells better then when all of us are having them. Father has the privelage of going into a shop and buy candies anytime. But not us.

Father's Clay Horse

By Anor

ONE day Father bought a tin of clay home. He said he wanted to make a clay horse. Soon he started his work.

Everyday when he is tired of writing that was the time when he was writing "The Importance of Living"; he worked on the pony that later it turned into a horse.

Father took a lump of clay and tried to make a head first. It was not very good. But he said that that was just a model and after he finished it he will give a last touch to it. After weeks and weeks the whole thing was done. Father said that now he is going to do some nice work to it.

At first Father thought of giving up, because it was no good. The horse's nose was as sideway as can be, and the feet won't stand. The body was not like the horse's. So the horse stood on the table for a week or so. But Father was idling when he was tired. Soon, somehow the horse was in the hands of Father again.

Father went to the Statue of Bolivar often to get the proportion right. The horse was better then, but not so good. Father went to the window of a wine shop and looked at the "White Horse." So the horse was more like one. Father asked for a creditsism. We all agree that the nose was not in its right place and one eye was lower then the other. Father stuck a bit of clay in the eye and made another one higher. The nose was in the right place now and everything was right. Father said that he wanted to make the lines of a horse show. There finally came a day that Father was satisfied with the horse. So he went on the paint to the green clay horse's body. The color was bronz. Father's hands were so dirty everytime he painted. But when he was dictating they were always clean. Not more then a week the horse was dry and stood on the table of the hall. Proud and manly.

One day an uninteresting freind came. Father was alway mad at them. So he took the excuse of working and went in his room. By closeing the door, he is free to do anything. So he took the horse again and painted it gold. Also he put his finger prints on it, to make sure that Lin Yutang made it. He put his name on the platform and the date too. So the bronz horse was turned into a gold one.

Feb 5, came. The horse was put in the trunk with many other things. Across the Atlantic Ocean through Italy, came to Menton and Out it came again. All frittered into little pieces on the legs.

Father put them together. The Golden horse was well again. One day on the mantelpiece it stood, someone bumped into it and the royal horse was limp. When we wanted to move to Paris Father could not make up his mind whether the horse's life should end or not. But mother made the disision by throwing the thing into the waste paper basket. So the horse was moved with all the wastes in spite of the finger prints Father made.

Father and His Food

By Anor

Father is well-known for being fond of roast beef already I suppose. His stomach is very good at dijestion. Father is so afraid of cold things. After a meal no fruits for him. In a cafe, coffee is the choice or tea. There is a long story about him being sick.

Father is so good at eating that even when he is sick he eats double of the amount he eats usually. He isn't the kind of people who is polite and say "I don't want anything," when he is really hungry. Just this morning Father asked me to get two pears for him. "That's how I get well" he says "by eating so much." Mother's arguement is that Father never gets anything serious, so he can eat so much. Father is not so greedy as it seems to be as one reads this. If you wake up and see a plate of orange skins or something of that sort, you can be sure that it isn't mother.

Mother never eats things when she hasn't washed her mouth. But Father sometimes doesn't wash his mouth when he is in a hurry. How Father can eat so much half is due to mother, who gives him so much care when Father has the slightest sickness. Half of the things are given by mother when father doesn't ask for any. And the rest are all father's wishes. If father says, "Beef soup taste very good," means already he wants some. Well father has a strange stomach. Though he eats the best of the things we have at home, he never gets fat. That's why mother wants to reduce to get even with father when they go out. But really mother isn't fat comparing to the Americans. But isn't fat also comparing to the Chinese. Father never swallows the smoke like the students do when they are forbidden to smoke.

Father's Childhood

By Anor

It is funny how a pastor's son can write the importance of living in to a book. Father who once when he was small said to grandmother "I am going to write a book so that the whole world will know me" has now full filled his wish. Father was borned in 1895 at Oct. 10. He is the fifth brother. And is the next to the smallest. Father sat one night while holding the pipe in his mouth and told us his whole story.

He went to school at ten years old with his brothers. Father said when he was small he did not think studying was a good thing for it was all too easy.

Once when they were having the examination father didn't prepare anything but asked a friend to go fishing. But the poor friend, the next day father got very good marks but the friend didn't.

In summer they used to wear torned shoes of which the toes came out and kicked the wooden balls, and without washing their hands they go to dinner. Sometimes they even go to the teacher's table at night and look at the questions for to-morrow so that they could prepare them. And the next day the teacher wondered why all the students got such good marks. All these things happened in father's childhood. Father said yet the most happy moment was after a year staying at school without seeing grandmother the day when they arrived at the door of the house they would cry and yell and shout for grandmother and ran to her bossom. Sometimes when the boat went too slow they even got up and ran on the shore for the impatient excitement and happiness. Father said another way to get home was to go quietly and hide in the house till Grandmother passed throught him and then rush out and embraced her. So father said they always had this problem at hand to decide. Another big problem was when the boat got half way, there was a stand where people ate pig's liver soup or fried noodles, each were ten cents and equally delicious. They then really had to decide which to take. If I were father I would take the noodles.

Speaking of father at school they each had a penny a week to spent. Father was very good at spending it. And he was more a good boy then he is now mother would think. For Father used part of the money for a HAIR-CUT! Imagine father going to a barber shop without any one pushing him! The rest of the penny father spent them in candies, of course that was a more natural thing for a boy to do of his age.

When father was graduated from the middle [school] Grandfather sent him to Shanghai, to St. John's University.

Father found out then what books meant and was a real good student. Then he got gold meddles every year till he had to stop himself to let others have a chance of getting them. Father was said to be the most naughty student in the Chinese class. But father explained that the Chinese teacher himself was so old fashioned that he said from China you can take a automobile and drive over to America and all the students dispiced him. Father bought English books into the Chinese class room and read English while the Chinese teacher taught. At that time father even took up the course of being a pastor and learned to preach till the bishop told him it was better for him not to be a pastor for the more father read the Bible the less father believed in it. He said that he never prepared the lessons in the Bible but when the bishop asked one thing father made up the stories for the man and made guesses. Sometimes his guess was right but some times Father made another different story out of the Bible.

Finally father graduated from college and was engaged to mother. Mother had waited four years for father to marry her till at last she said to herself, "This Yutang, he engaged me for four years already, but why doesn't he come and marry me?"

At last at 1919 they were married. But I was dissapointed when I asked them later for the wedding picture that mother said, "We took some but when we handed the film to the brother of Y.T.'s he put it in his pocket and the pocket had a hole and so he lost it." I was saddened by this answer but I could imagine the picture!

After marrying they went to U.S.A. to study. Father studied at Havard and got every course "A". Then they went to Germany to study. They stayed at a pension. Mother told us that one day when they took the laundry out to be washed and found a tail sticking out of the bag and father pulled it out and fond a mouse alive! Mother was so frightened by the sight of the longtail and father through into the toilet.

Mother had appendise in Germany and went to the hospital. They were then very poor. The days when mother was in hospital they had only $13.00 in the pocket and father only ate oatmeal for the day which cost only 5¢ a package which will last for days. Then they telegramed to China to ask for money.

One day when mother went to the doctor and the doctor said that maybe mother wouldn't be able to give birth to any children. You ought to see how mother cried, although I never saw it myself! But then when mother had Adet in Germany father said, "we better go back for Adet might be a German." So they bought the boat ticket. The very day they sailed father went and tested for his Ph.D. Mother was so worried for if Father didn't pass the test what should they do? Father told mother that if others could pass the test why cant he? At last at twelve o'clock that day mother waited at the road and the professor came with father and said he had passed with honour! Mother was so glad that she kissed father right on the road. Then they sailed for China. They arrived at Amoy and Adet was out at May 6th and cried every afternoon as a regular habit till Grandfather was angry. At Peking I was borned and Mother said I was the fattest girl out of the eighteen in the hospital. Then at Shanghai Meimei was borned and at 1936 we came to U.S. and now we are in France.

[*But if I am borned in 1936 I am just 2 years old.—Meimei*]

Father and the Old Gold Contest

By Anor

THE Old Gold contest was so popular in New York that father once was in it. First he thought of buying their cigarettes but later when we knew we could draw the cover of the package, all of us helped to draw. $100,000 for the first price. Of course anyone would like to get the amount of money.

Day and night father worked on it, he even took the trouble of going to the Columbia library and find out. We all were sure that at least we could get $10.00. Father didn't want to use his name, so we made the name "Miss Lin Yu Ju". Mother throught father was crazy and didn't think he would win at all. But father said "If other's can win why not I. I am not below averge." So we children helped father draw the covers and guess the thing out.* Later when some one put the answers out for 50¢ each Father bought it and found out that only two were wrong. So he started another name. We had to draw about fifty covers. One night we took them all out and drew till ten o'clock. There was one answer that father throught he was right and the man in Boston that put the answers out for money was wrong. Father, therefore mailed the last week's contest to the Old Gold company. It was so exciting. We waited for the letter from Old Gold to say the $100,000 were ours. After a month or so the answers were out in the paper. 1000 men got the first prise. So they had to tie again. We looked for Lin Yuju's name. But——n—o——. Nothing about Lin Yuju. We therefore looked for the answers and found out that only one was w—r—o—n—g. Father got so disappointed. And it tought father that writing books was more sure to make money than contests.

* *Not me.—Meimei*

When Father Gives a Speech

By Anor

Father often gives speeches in clubs or halls or anything of that sort. If he gets money from them he would feel a little better but still he hates them. I sometimes think how can he write so fast. If the appointment were at eight o'clock he doesn't have to prepare it a week earlier and practice it in his study, he just takes a walk at 5:30 and comes back and has a foot bath then at seven he sits at his desk and thinks for a while then shuts his door and tipe the out lines out and at eight he is ready. At the same time mother gets ready and out they go.

Once when we were on "President Hoover" they told him to give a lecture. And we kids went to listen too as on the boat we could get in and out as we wished to. Many waiters in the boat came up too and felt quite proud to serve father at meals. When he began many persons looked at us and we felt quite embaressed. When father got through people applauded and mother told us not to because after all he is our father and we can't be too proud. So mother never applauds when at the public but comes home and congratulates him.

It *is* a strange feeling when we listen to father. Sometimes when he talks about something serious his face would get red and it seems that father is very "manly". He never gets stage fright or anything. There must be something in father that never stops. Often people tells him to lecture without his knowing beforehand, but father can go on and talks endless.

Often before father sets out for the speech mother would come to his study and say tenderly, "Y.T. comb your hair." Father would smile at her and take the comb. Sometimes when he is thinking during the meal he would get up in the middle of the dinner and type. Sometime he does make one feel dizy by walking from his study to the dining room and from the dining room to the study. So strange a man is father.

A Hair-Cut You Must Have, Y.T.

By Anor

Mother: Y.T., you must have a hair-cut.

Father: No! It is all right. I've never seen a man so neat as I am.

Mother: But it *is* too long. You go and look at the mirror.

F.: Now you see? It is not too long. I am too neat for an author.

"A HAIRCUT YOU MUST HAVE. Y.T."

M.: Y.T., you ought to know yourself that the hair is long.

F. But I just had a haircut two weeks ago. I am not going until I myself think it is too long. I am forty-three.

M. Forty-three is forty-three but your hair is long.

F. I am going to have my hair dressed like Mr. X. As long as his, and not put any tonic on like him, and not to comb it every day.

M. Please, listen to me. You are going to lucture to-morrow night. I will be ashamed to see you on the platform with such long hair.

F. And I too shall be ashamed to let the audence see that Lin Yutang's hair is so neat.

M. Put your coat on. There is a barbor on the 84th St. It's near.

F. I know it. But I am not going to give any business to them.

The Next Day

M. Are you going to the barbar's?

F. No, I have to prepare my lucture.

M. No, please go after lunch.

F. Oh! I have to sleep after lunch.

M. Then go when you take a walk in the afternoon.

F. Please, I am not your son.

M. But you are.

F. But I am not.

M. Now, Y.T. Don't argue. Go.

F. In order to have peace I will go.

M. Oh, yes, surely you are. Don't forget to let them sampoo it. It is dirty. And tell them to cut it about half a inch.

F. All right, Hong.

M Thank you.

Father and His Pipe

By Anor

THE pipe that Father uses is used for everything. First, of course, he smokes it. On the round end of the pipe, where he puts the tobacco in is used for wiping his nose. That end is always hot, because the tobacco is always burning. Father's nose is always very oilly. And the warm warm pipe is so soothing to the nose. So Father often wipes his nose with the pipe. Therefore the one end of the pipe is filled with Father's oil from the nose. On the other end where he puts it in his mouth is used in pointing things. He points the menu with it and nocks the chair nails with it. The pipe is to be cleaned everyday. The tobacco oil is always so smelly and black. Sometimes when Father doesn't be careful, the oil gets in his mouth, then he says it tastes bitter, and spids all over the corners of the streets.

Father says he can't do anything without his pipe. Once in a while when he puts his pipe away or doesn't know where it is he won't do anything but walk about the whole house and says, "My pipe! where is my pipe? pipe, pipe." He always can find it and laughs and be satisfied. Father is always mad at his dearest pipe. He says, "I filled this pipe an hour ago and till now I haven't even lighted it." Then when he has time to smoke and he would say, "Now! May I do a thing? Smoke the pipe?" This is always asked. But not until we have answer him he is already smoking.

Father Makes Fun of Mother

By Anor

"OH! Hong, my purse—" father said sadly. Mother knew what had happened. She still pretended to be cheerful but her heart had sunk down and said, "you have lost it." "My purse," repeated father. "My purse." Mother was possitive that Father had lost his purse. Father continued, "My purse, my purse," then Father turned into a half smiling face, and said, "My purse, Hong, can't be put into the new coat pocket." "Y.T. You have been fooling me for eighteen years." Of course Mother was glad that the purse wasn't lost. Father had a good laugh and said, "Look it's too big for the pockets." "Now it's time to go to Thomas Cook." Thus father went out.

"Aha!" said mother "somebody forgot his tobacco pouch!" We all laughed when father went and said "Somebody has forgotten his tobacco pouch," After a long while father came in and said, "Isn't it easy for me to find out that I forgot something?" "What?" said mother, "Oh then I have lost it." Mother smiled to us. "What?" mother repeat while I was holding the pouch behind my hands. "My tobacco pouch. I have lost it." "Now, Y.T. you big boy. You always lost things. Where did you put it?" "I don't know," Father exclaimed. Then we all laughed. "I don't know where *is* your thing." As I was holding it in front of his eyes. "Yes, Yes, Yes! I don't know!" While father took it from my hands and immediately he fealed his pipe.

The Short History of My Name

By Anor

MY regular name is not "Anor" but "Lin Woo Shuang". When we came to America my parents decided that they'd better call me Anor for they DON'T know how to pronounce my Chinese name properly and each one would call me a different name when they see the spelling of my Chinese name.

I hate people calling my name wrong as they call Chiang Kai Chek. A French teacher said, "So your leader is 'Chang Ching Chec*k*' ". We Chinese had to laugh secretly and wanted to laugh out loud but are not supposed to. Every foriegner, especially in America, doesn't dare say Chiang Kai Shek loud for he knows that he cant pronounce it right and pauses a little before saying his name and says it in a low voice. They pronounce that *K* on the end too much so that his name sounds ridiculous. In Chinese the name is pronounced very different from what they say in America and Europe.

How my parents named me "Anor" was not recently for "Anor" was my milk name. Mother always gives us strange names for a milk name. The reason why they all call me Anor is one day as we were in Peking, I went to a park. I sat there and a Foreign boy came to me and said, "No, no, no, no, no," I did not know what it meant but I kept on saying, "No, no, no, no, no" when I came back and every day said "No, no, no, no, no." So Mother called me Ano for the Chinese always add "A" pronounced in French like ah, (Many people call me A-nor (in U.S.) So I was named Ano, for a long time till I came to U.S.A. But my name was not yet complete and the "R" at the end had not come yet.

So the history of "R" was built in America. A man asked father what were our names and father said, "Adet—Ano'R' and Meimei," for father thought "Ano" sounded not so good so R came walking along at the end.

So my name was built letter by letter and it is complete now, I hope, but any day any letter might come jumping along in any place among "ANOR".

I don't like very much the name Anor for it is neither foriegn nor Chinese. But I'd rather have Anor then a foriegn name. It would seem ridiculious to me to have any Chinese bearing names like,

Violet, Rose, Evelyn, Mary, Margrat, Daisy, Lily, Iris, Patsy or anything else. I ask you would it seem strange to call father

George Lin, John Lin, Richard Lin, Dick Lin, Charles Lin, or even Edward Lin?

Many people call father "Mr. Yu-Tang, how do you do, and Mrs. Yu-tang how are you?" We laughed at them for having the privelage of changing our family name. But at the same time we can't blame them for not knowing that we Chinese put our Family Name first which is more sensible and correct. Speaking about correctness, the envolopes in China are more right also. I mean the way they write addresses on the envolopes, it is like

France
Paris
59 Rue Nicolo
Mr. Lin Yutang

It is easier for the post office to see first what country and city it is step by step before the name. Now in U.S. and Europe it is just the contrary, from bottom up!

Talking back about names I allow any one to call me by Chinese name in case any one can pronounce it correctly, if not *Anor* is better. But I will not have one single name like Rose or Betty or anything.

Chinese names have a meaning which the West dont. Woo Shuang in Chinese means no pair in the world, in other words, the only one.

Chinese Words in My Name

By Anor

This is a paragraph about my name in Chinese writing. We have all forms of writing. The Chinese

words come some of them from the meaning and others from shape. For example:

woods

Lin, our family name means woods—where there are many trees. It is made of two trees.

a tree

This is one part of the word *Lin.* And it means a tree and when we write two of them it means the forest of the woods.

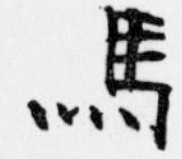

This is "ma" meaning horse. The four dots down here are supposed to be the four legs. In the olden times they didn't write it just like this but made it some what like a horse.

These are two of the originals. They look like horses.

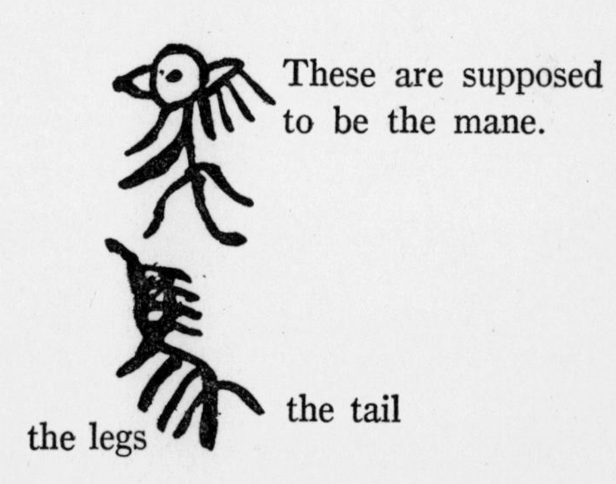

These are the 38 ways of writing my name

They are not used now but these words are old. Collected on stones and grave stones and seals, too.

These two we use now.

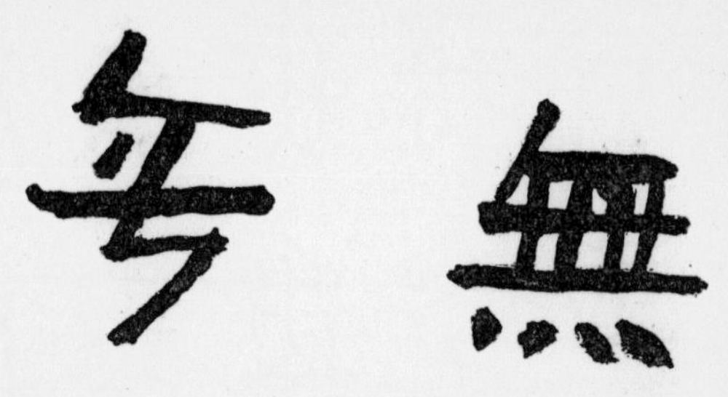

We have many of the parts but no alphabet. The parts we put together to make a word. So we have more interesting words than the West. My name is *Woo Shuang*. It means no pair and *Shuang* is written

 and it means *pair* (of birds).

This 又 is supposed to be a hand and the two above mean two birds and two birds resting on a hand is a pair.

We have curios names which have meaning. Adet is *"Ju su"* meaning in French *"comme ca"* and mine you know.

Rats and Mice at Home

By Anor

It is, I know, not a very dignifing thing to talk about rats at our apartment. But nevertheless it is interesting to see how Lin Yutang catches a rat!

American apartments have rats too! Well, in U.S. we have to catch the rats ourself. It was in C.P.W. The old house which had not been repeared since long.

There came suddenly a squeak and something black with a long tail ran over the sitting room, "Ah, it's a mouse!" Meimei cried aloud and certainly it was!

"Pa, Pa, there's a mouse in this room!" we all cried to father. And now father came hurrying from his chair, threw his pipe down and come stamping on the floor. "A rat! A rat, it's in Ma's room now!"

So father took a broom stick and a poker in the fire place and ran to the room. He closed all the doors first and asked that who wanted to come in and help him to fight? Of course Adet can't be it for all she can do in these moments was to LAUGH. Meimei and Mother are scared of mice, so I was the only one left. I was interested in the Adventure, so I went in quick and closed the door. We two went on hunting in the room and father threatened it by beating the stick on the floor

They three heard the great rattling in the room and we heard laughing and shoutings and stampings outside the room. Now do we get anywhere with the mouse? I should say not. But where has the mouse gone to? So with great disappointment we searched for the mouse. Ah, but it is in the bath room! So the hero told me not to come in for the bath room would be too crowded. So he again closed the bath room door and the mouse didn't have much place to hide. But father made a lot of noise, yes, indeed he did.

After all a mouse is a mouse and Father is Father and with a whip the mouse's head was hit by father.

"I've got it, I've got it," father came dancing out

with the mouse upon the stick. We all laughed at the dance father did for he imitated the girls in Radio City. One foot down and the other up with his hand on the waist and the other holding his enemy.

"Where are we going to throw it?" Meimei asked anxiously. Mother replied calmly, "Of course in the toilet." "But suppose the falsh toilet doesn't work?" "Dont worry," was the reply.

So down went the mouse. After that there was a lot of conversation made.

"It was even bigger then the last one we caught."

"Its tail was as long as this!"

"It was a fat one."

"I thought Father'd never catch it."

"It is a easy thing."

"I hope there isn't any more."

etc.

There is another story about Father and another mouse. A very interesting story.

Again there was a mouse in the U.S. apartment. This is a very pitiful story.

A mouse rather then a rat was running across the hall. Father used the carpet cleaner to beat it or something and unfortunately the poor mouse was stuck half between the thing for at first the mouse was in the part where the dirt was in the carpet cleaner. Father tried to open the cover and half between father loose hold of it and the poor little innocent mouse was stuck half between, alive! Father tried to kill it but didn't dare to. The pair of small round eyes looked at father as if to think,

"You men, why do you beat me? I came to do you

no harm. I don't understand. Mercy upon me, I want my parents!"

This look softened Father's heart. I still remember very vividly the very look of it, squeaking unbearably to ask for relief. The very look of it made him a handsome rat. And now—what was to do with it? We couldn't bare to kill it. It would be a very cruel thing to do after his look and if you let him go you couldn't

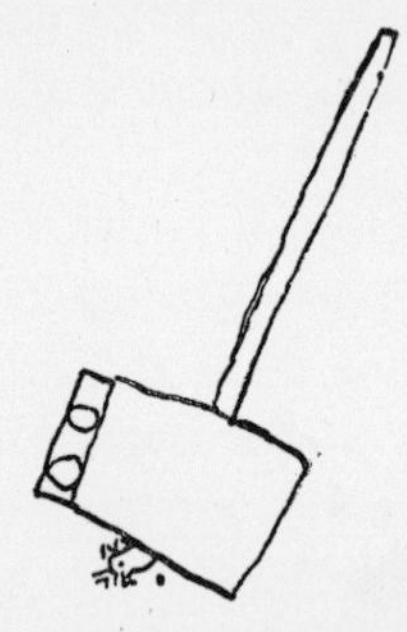

THE POOR MOUSE

and if you let him go he is already wounded and will suffer. There came a great problem to this.

WHAT TO DO WITH THIS MOUSE?

Let it be your business to answer it? What would you do? Every way seems wrong and yet you can't leave the poor mouse just like that squeaking with sorrow. What do you think you'd do? I just ask you then tell you what we did.

Have you figured it out? What we did was to ring the back elivater bell and ask for a man to come up. Then we told him all about the story and told him to take it down and let him do what ever he wants with it boil it or fry it or bake it with some baking powder and we wish never to see that unbearable face again.

Father said, "To catch a mouse and kill a mouse or any other thing has its hard and easy way to do. For instance, I dare catch that mouse just without that look, plain, beat it without thinking before or even consider him, just say you have to. That is the easy way and one dares to it. The hard way is to consider it before Yourself. Just think how innocent that mouse was and have you got the heart to kill it?"

After the handy man was gone we found in the kitchen a little blood and one fifth of the mouse's foot left on the ground.

Now you can't clean it up with a broom so that the broom has a few drops of mouse blood on it, you can't take a cloth and take it up and then wash the mouse's blood with soap it would seem ridiculous.

So finally the family confrience ended and the thing was to wrape the little foot up with newspaper and throw it into the garbage can.

But don't you think that the thing was not quite yet solved. WHO WAS TO WRAPE IT?

You can't elect for it'd be unfair for the person. So we choose voulenteer. Adet was the good girl and she took it and wrapped it nicely up and it went to the garbage!

[*I am scared of little things like mice and worms.—Meimei*]

Singing at Home

By Adet

SINGING is the thing father and I can not do. As father said, "I can accomplish many things and can be a tailor, shoeshiner, writer, actor if necessary, but singing is what I can't do. I haven't got a manly base and neither lady's serprina", I think it is quite true. Father can play the piano pretty well and mother has a full high voice. She was once a member of Songster's Club.

After dinner that night father picked up some pieces from "The world's master pieces" and played them as an enjoyment. "Come on, Hong. Just "hum" or "la" this tune." "O.K." responded mother and she walked toward the piano and put one of her arms around father's neck. The children just skipped over to the piano. Anor was beside mother, and as the family said that she has a nice voice, she followed the singing very womanlike. Meimei couldn't catch up so she just stood by and looked. I couldn't sing so I stood by and looked. When I saw that they were going toward a high note then I sang, trying to make my voise as broken as possible and everybody laughed and told me to shut up. Meimei then said she wanted to go to the toilette and I had to accompany her. The other three could then do their music peacefully. In a little moment we two came trotting along, and as we came near the piano we instantly changed the trotting into a tip-toe walking for they were singing awfully seriously.

Mother's voice is really good, I am sure if she has a singing teacher she can develop her singing very well. Anor never really sings as loud as she talks. When she sings she always has her mouth very pointed. I always tell her to sing out loud like when she argues, but she hasn't tried yet.

Then father said, "let me play 'Jack Horner' for Meimei." And then Meimei was put on the chair and there she sang. The others all sang lowly in order to hear Meimei's singing. From Jack Horner we swiched to "The Farmer in the dell". We all sang including father and me. Father sang real loud and he imitated the manly base and then "Lily Pons". We all laughed so loud.

Then the father told mother to sing "Now the day is over" and told me to play. I was impatient and handicap in playing piano. I kept mother waiting for the note to come. Then I said, "father better play it." And everybody *quite* agreed. Then father played and mother sang.

A little while later father asked mother and Anor to "hum" "Minuite in G". They did and while Meimei and I tried to imitate the minuit dance. It was pretty good and then Anor wanted to join us. We had a three man minuite and then as we bowed to each other we knocked our head. It was painful and then everyone retired to the sitting room.

Our Plays

By Adet

I DON'T know how we started out on this idea of acting. I suppose it came from the encouragement of our parents. We give plays almost once a week for a season, and after the season we shall be tired of these things and forget about it for a few months and then start it again.

Father and mother always enjoy our plays and as for others I do not think they would understand them.

In an idle afternoon, Anor and Meimei would think of preparing a play for the evening after dinner. I usually do not like the finding of material and the rehearsing and so I often refuse and almost every time I have to yield to them, otherwise they will be miserable for that after noon. As soon as I consent, we have to start thinking on what we shall play. Usually we give several scenes of our friends; each one imitates a character and show the characteristic of that person. Then we make out the conversation which was really said by these people. Of course we use interesting characters. When all this is thought out, and it takes quite a long time, we choose our parts. Often we would fight for a certain role and then settle it by drawing sticks. When it comes to the rehearsing part I usually tell Meimei what to do. We rehearse twice for each scenes, the first time we plan out the positions and dialogues and the second and last time we time how many minutes we shall take. Of course there are alway shouting out new ideas and talking at the same moment which nobody can hear in the rehearsals.

Well, about the costumes. We sometimes have them and sometimes don't. When we do have them, we use all kinds of things. Mother's bathrobe, Father's necktie, scarfs, rubbers and overalls, etc. We like to have costume on, but the cleaning up after the play is always a nuisance to everybody. So often we just go without them.

Anor and Meimei always make the programs and they are generally very pretty.

After a little rest when dinner is eaten, we start our plays. Before we start we are laughing already either at our costumes or at the roles. Trying to control our laughter, we come out and introduce ourselves and we say "One, two, three, our play is on." The acting sometimes is good, often before I start that sentence we all burst into laughter. When I laugh I can't do anything except sit on the floor and laugh, and laugh till my tears come out.

After it is over we start the play over again. Meimei is always the serious one whenever there is acting; she would tell us two to shut up laughing. Father and mother are the only audence and they all laugh at something funny and our immutuarity. Once I was supposed to carry Meimei in my arm to Anor. It was a very funny part. I bursted into laughter again and Meimei and I both fell on the ground. Fortunately we didn't hurt ourselves. Later I had to change parts with Anor and let her carry Meimei. We all act pretty well usually and the parents always laugh during our play.

Those Crazy Hats

By Anor

THAT day father bought a magazine, and in it were all sorts of crazy hats. They used a dusting brush, a mould for baking cake, a kind of vegetable, some rolls for lunch, etc. for a hat and on it were ribbons tied beautifully on them. I think they would be pretty if they were original but since you know that the rolls are for eating and the brush is for dusting the house they look ridiculous on a fashionable lady.

So we kids decided that night to invent each one a crazy hat as crazy as possible and let father judge which one is the best for mother was not at home.

So each one went into a private corner where no one

could see her until she was ready. So we tried to collect all the crazy things for a hat.

The resorts were that the first time Adet's hat got the first prize and the second time I did.

Adet was crazy enough to put a gramaphone record on the head with a dish cloth hanging down from the ear with a washing brush on the other side of the ear were pens and pencils sticking out of the hair. That time I had a embrodary on my head and on top of it was a saucepan. Meimei had books on her head and pens, pencil, paper, all the things needed in a study were on her head.

Then the next time Adet's hat had the most kinds of spoons on her hat with each one sticking out.

I had a heavy wastepaper basket and beneath it was a soft cousion and in between stood the rubber doll of Meimei's. Meimei had a bag for marketing on with a spoon hanging on her ear.

After that contest I told Adet that really it was easy to be a fashionable lady for all the crazy hats were not any better the those we had that night. I also said that when the whole world was really crazy and mad they could have hand-lights for a hat and when the light shines down to her face they would be able to see her face at night. She added that when the face was fit for what color she can have that color light shinning on her face. We thought that it was a very good idea and that the world was really crazy enough, to have that kind of hat for a change.

Then Adet after a minute's thinking spoke again and said that after all one could make a dress all of vegetables and fruits. Then I thought what this future world would be like after centries. It must be a great difference. They might take us, our dresses and think what a wonder it was to wear these dress in the 20th centry time.

And I had a carot for my cigarette with a basket for a hat.—Meimei

Father Points at Things

(Food, Dress, Girls, Education and Others)

By Anor

I WILL make Father talk with one of us and tell us all about the things above.

F. Adet, this dish tastes very nice, doesn't it?

A. Yes, I always like the Chinese food better.

F. Good, you are right! In American or any European food you just have a big peice of meat and cut, cut, and cut. Not enough vegetable, but potato. They have to eat the bread quite a lot in order to belance. That's why I hate Foreign food.

A. Yes.

F. And in Chinese food you can put a piece of meat that is enough for only one person in American food into many dishes and mix with others. And if a guest comes you don't nessarily have to add anything for him. But in Foriegn food you had to add another potion.

A. Yes that is right. Which would you prefer, boy or girl? *

* *Since I am a girl I prefer to be a girl and if I am a boy I prefer to be a boy, if I am a boy I don't know if I am a bad boy or a good boy.—Meimei*

F. Of course I want to be a boy or a man. It seems to me that women have more trouble then man. For instance, in the world, more men are well-known than women, more men earn money than women. Men don't have such sickness as women do. If something happens women are always shyer than man. Women cares for sociaty, and what people think of her. Men don't have to care for sociaty, can live without it. But women have to be careful of everything they say because of sociaty.

A. I too prefer to be a boy.

F. In your young age I always say to you girls are luckier than boys because they have a beautiful dresses to wear, but boys wears grey, white, black and brown for the corlors. Of course a child at the age of from three to six or seven would think so. But when they grow up they will know without anybodie's telling.

A. Speaking about dress, of course, women have more good ones.

F. That you don't have to mention. But anyway there is no use defending girls are luckier than boys.

A. Oh, I am not, but which would you want, Chinese dress or European?

F. Well, each has his own goodness. As to man, I would certainly want Chinese dress. A long gown that hangs down from your shoulder. In side it is like a suit of pajamers. But look at the foreign dress. An under wear that sticks on your skin, a shirt, and jacket and the coat. On your neck there comes a thing that ties you like a dog, which is called a "colar" and a necktie like the dog chain to tie tight on your neck. Isn't it silly or crazy? If a fat man wears a foreign dress it is like this, his stomach that sticks out in the middle of it there ends the shirt just right in the mids of the stomach in the air. Then the trousers comes to meet the shirt and use a belt to hold it on, you think how would the trousers stay on?

A. Ha! Ha! right. But how about women?

F. Foreign dresses have more to change. You can wear many kinds. But Chinese dresses don't. Just the same I am going to be a women dressmaker, and design dresses for ladies. I am going to change the Chinese dress into many different styles.

Meimei's Collection in Stamps

By Anor

ONE day in a 5 and 10¢ store father bought a 500 package of stamps for 20¢, hoping that we, Adet and I would get interested in them. The next day Adet and I sat on the floor and sort out different countries. Meimei came and looked, then she sat down with us, then she helped us to tear the paper from the stamps, then she helped us to sort the stamps. She came step by step. "Meimei, don't do anything to the stamps, because you might not know them," we ordered. But day by day we forget about the stamps and Meimei took them out every day when we don't play with them. After a few weeks father saw that the stamps had become Meimei's, so father bought more and more for her. In a short while the stamp album was full. Father bought a bigger book for her. One day we found Meimei knowing country names like Hejaz, Afghanistan, Nicaragua, Porto Rica, Salvador, Somali Coast, etc. And Father tought her where they were in. Now she can memerrize the countries by heart. I will tell her to say where the countries are "From Mexico down it is Honduras, Guatemala, Salvador, Nicaragua." All the places where no one in the family but Father and her know where and what they are. In her play time she would go counting the stamps. Up to now she has about 1300 stamps. But I don't have confidence in her because everytime she counts the stamps become less and less. Today she says it is 1256 stamps but yesterday it was 1389. If not counting her stamps she would go from page to page taking a tune like "Mary had a litter lamb" and instead of singing the word she would take the names of the countries and sing them. For instance Luxemburg, ah Luxemburg, Luxemburg, etc. Right now I can hear her sitting on the toilet singing her stamps by the tune of "Mary had a litter lamb." Sometimes we would take a stamp and say, it is a blue stamp and on it there are two knights fighting. She would immediately say it is an Italian stamp. Even in the hard countries she can know them. If you turn a page and say what is the country on next page? she can answer correctly.

The first book is a big red book. The second and third are green ones. All together she has three books now and can resight almost every stamp. If in a shop window has stamps in them, we would fool her "Meimei has no interest in this shop at all." Then she would know that it is STAMPS.

[*I count I will say* 51 52 53 54 55 56 58 59 30 *so I count them I know it is no use of counting them.* —*Meimei*]

I Like to Have a Room

By Anor

I WISH I could have a room as I like to have it. It is not too small or to big, but with lots of windows. A bed that is very low and soft, a big table of my own and no one can look in and see how dirty or unneat it is but me. I wish to have a piano, a small one for me to play on when I feel lonesome and a sofa that is also low and soft. On the wall I would like to have pictures of my parents and sisters. The room must be full of sun, the sofa placed right near the window. A dirty smock for me to wear when I feel I am too clean. I like the room full of mirrors. On my table there lays a box of pencils and colored pencils, old and new, beside it there are some good drawing papers. In the middle of the desk stands many of my favorite books with beautiful glass book stands one on each side. I wish to have a big draw. One side of it is very neat but the other old and dirty. In the corner of the room there is a rocking chair very uncomfortible, a wooden one, and when I sit on it it would make a lot of noise and about to break but can't break. I'd sit on it just for fun and to frighten myself. The floor is to be very bright so that I can sligh on it and sometimes I would fall. Around the bed are many shelfs and a light for me to read at night. An old clock on the wall and sings when it's time. A wardrobe made of swell wood and inside hang some of my beautiful and ugly dresses. A couple of Mexican dolls, not for playing but hanged on the wall with gray background. Speak of the colors I want my wall to be light gray, very light. Out side the windows I see many tall big trees and near my window is an orange tree so that when the wind blows I could get some oranges. On the floor there is a piece of glass so that I could look down and down there is the dining room so that when my parents are having guests I could look down and see how they look but they can't see me.

Well, if all my *abarrations* come true I would be more than satisfied and contented.

P.S. Also I want a very good knife on the desk, not to use it but to look at it, and a typewriter, a small one.

Religion

By Adet

THIS morning I was early as usual; got up before anyone. So I took breakfast alone; later on father joined me. The first question he asked was: "Do you believe in god?" I was quite surprised and didn't know how to find an answer for it. I said, "What do you mean?" Then he started, "When I was about your age I also got up very early and felt fine in the morning. I was very religious at that time, often I would read a chapter for the Bible. What do you think of god now?" I was forced to give a reply. I said, "Well, I never thought of this question, for when I do think about it it gets all mixed up. But in general I say I am not a Christian or Buddist." I continued, "Do you want me to return, not exactly return, to religion?" I was in quite a muddle, for father usually talks to us against religion. He replyed, "No, I am just asking."

Meanwhile mother came in. She asked for coffee. I poured half cup for her and took the pot away. She asked for more and I told her to take milk. She took but little milk and then I had to give her the coffee. She doesn't want to drink too much milk in order not to get fat. I tried to prevent her from doing so, but I failed. Then we somehow switched the subject to Chinese English-writers and talked about J. W. etc., and then from J. W. to modern politicions like Y.M. Father pointed out that all the modern Chinese officials need is social abilities. Father said mother would be a very good deplomatic's wife. Mother smiled and said, "Yes, I am sure. But I never have the ambition of father being a politician. I even opposed it." Father said, "Indeed this is true, I must give you credit for it."

After breakfast father went to his study and I happened to go in. Then father continued his discourse about "God". I said, "There is no god in the world." "But it is not purely machanic." "Why not?" I said. "Of course every thing can be anylized by science, but where did the origin of life come from, no one can calculate. It is misterious. We satisfy ourselves by calling it "God" as the taoists call it Tao. Taoist's philosophy is just fitted for the scientists, for science and this philosophy come together." This was explained and I went to my room and started my work.

Part II. AMERICA

The Day We Left Shanghai

By Anor

August 1, that excited day came! We were going to leave Shanghai! In the morning, I was the first one to wake up. I looked at Meimei and she smiled to me. In a little while Mother woke up, and then the rest. Mother got so nervous and excited and glad. At 10:00 many freinds came. Our room was full of guests and smoke and noise. Mother babbled to the ladies and Father to the men. After this one was gone the other came. We three children were so busy at opening the gifts. I was the most excited one among all. "Oh, it is a box of candy." "It's a box of crakers." "A dozen of handkerchiefs." "Oranges!" We kept on yelling. My voice was so loud and high that everyone could hear me. Meimei jumped up and down. Adet wanted both, hear mother talking with the fomen friends or see us opening the packages. But all the talking among the friends and relatives were almost the same. For instance, "No, the gifts are nothing, just a little thing for the kids." "And you must write to us—" "Take care of yourselfs—" etc. all mother could say was "Thank you" All these politeness made me sick. The whole morning was spent like this. At lunch we had many uninvited guests. After the lunch a friend of ours came and Father and him slept together in our room with snorings. While a friend that was going in the same boat with us went with us (mother and us three) to the old part of the city and mother was looking for a jade braslet. Some were too good and some too cheap. In a hot noon day in summer we walked for one hour or so that all were so thirsty, and yet didn't buy anything. When we got to the hotel it was an hour before we started for America. Mother and us three ordered each half melon, it was icy cold and we all had a good time with them. Then when we went up to our room, we found the friend taking a bath. We all laughed and laughed at his frankness. Father said such and such friends came and we were all excited again, remembering that we were going to America. Many of our friends came again and we all had tea. I still remember that I had cocoa. You know how hot it was, but maybe you don't. Mother forced me to drink it because the first meal on board was always not so good and that I might get hungry as I usualy do. I could jump to the sky because I was so glad and excited I couldn't drink or eat a thing. But instead I kept walking, jumping, stooping on the floor around the table. Everybody told me to stop it. But I couldn't, my hands were all cold and I laughed and told father, "we are nearly going to start". Somehow with great difficulty I drank my cocoa down. Then a friend of ours called a taxi and we all went in. At that time I was so glad because we were really going. Our taxi was with two big baskets of flowers. In a minute we got to the station. There was a whole lot of people standing near the sea. We all broke in-to laughter. A friend lent us a boat to drive to the steamer. All of the friends came on the little boat.

It was about 6 o'clock. The wind was warm and nice, we could see far away there stood "Pres.

Hoover". I never went in a real steamer before. But I was in an immense excitement. The steamer left at 11:00 in the night. We had each a glass of lemon juce. We were not acquaited with American waiters, all felt so strange. The friend began to go back one by one. Not until eight o'clock were they all gone. It was a lucky thing that no one cried. If any did I couldn't help from laughing, to be so rude.

The first thing we found in the boat at our rooms

were flowers. The rooms were full of flowers. We could hardly open the doors. We didn't want the flowers so much. So we put them in the dinning rooms. They occupied the whole space for putting flowers. And no one else could put anything on the table. We had about thirty big and small baskets.

In the rooms they were full of gifts. We had about 18 boxes of candies. At last the boat left, and we left China! But nobody knows when we were coming back again.

In Honolulu

By Anor

Across the big ocean to America, we stopped at Hawaii for a day. It was very exciting. The steamer landed very early in the morning before we woke. A bell-boy went around all the cabins calling people. up at seven. All of the passengers got up for the doctor and to stamp the passport. At ten o'clock, a man came and brought us two big flower rings for

us to wear on the neck as the custom is like that there. Mother let us wear them, but nobody wanted to,* and could through it away. So after all Adet and I had them. Then after half an hour waiting on the deck, more and more people came. We had never been to Hawaii before, and I don't know why about twenty people came and met us at the station, even

* *I got a head egg when they put those flower rings on me. There were lots of them and that was too much.—Meimei*

a camera man came and took a flash light of us, to our great dislike, espacially me. After we arrived at a new friend's home we five had at least thirty flower rings on our necks. Father and mother espacially they each had about eight that their necks were not long enough to hold them. When we got to the friend's home it was about two. Everyone took the rings off but left the most beautiful one on. Father's neck didn't enjoy being accompanied by so many flowers. We had Chinese food at lunch. There were three interesting things done or seen on that day. One was we went in a glass bottom boat, and saw the beautiful fish going and coming, full of colors, red, blue, green, purple, etc. And one kind of coral that was so rare to see. It had many colors and beautiful branches spreading out. Second, it was the Hawain dinner. Everything was cold. We sat on a long table. First two girls came and danced for us and put rings on us again. Then came the sort of "dinner" which to me was not dinner. They had a kind of soup that looked like cream. It was all right. But the trouble was that they didn't use any spoon. But dipped a FINGER in and put it in your mouth. So we didn't try any of the "soup". There were raw fish like the Japs have. So we didn't try any of the "fish". The table was decorated with leaves instead of the table cloth. There were many what they called "good Hawain things" which we didn't dare to eat. But "I think I didn't have enough!" said all of us when we got to the steamer again.

Third, there came a nice Hawaian food. A big crab which was one foot not counting the feet. That satisfied all of us as we had it in our cabin. Father couldn't break it so he finally put it in between the chase-of-draw and cracked it by pushing the draw in. Then the crab was cracked and the knob of the draw was broken. Anyway the crab saved us from hunger. Each with a handful of crab meat as we looked out the cabin windows. The sea breezes blew on our faces, the music played and we soothingly left the Flower Islands and to the big ocean again we sailed.

A Visit to Hollywood

By Anor

As we came from San Francisco to New York we passed through Hollywood. My parents, one day, went to see many of the movie stars. To our great disappointment we didn't go. It was seven o'clock at night when they came back. Mother told us all about the stars they met. Jeanette MacDonald, William Powell, Paul Lucas, Jean Hallow, Melvyn Douglas and some others. My parents saw Jeanette McDonald acting "Maytime" with the other stars and had a picture taken with her which was nice, also one with Paul Lucas.

Then one day we all went to visit Shirley Temple. It was the day we wanted to leave for New York. So we only talked with her for about ten minutes. But it was very worthwhile. At ten o'clock, there came a car. In it sat Shirley Temple, her mother, and two guards, a driver and a nurse. She had her little cute dressing house. Opposit the house was Janet Gayners'. Three or four camermen were waiting to take her picture with us. Shirlev Temple waved to us in the car. She came out and many people helped her to take her coat off. She is not spoiled at all, being so well-known. Shirley said two or three sentences of Chinese to us, which she was learning for her play "Stole Away". In a little while we had to go and catch the train. If not we could see her act.

Then before that day we went with our friend to take a drive. There we saw Claudet Colbert's house and Mary Picford's too. I guess that was all.

In New York we met two more well-known stars. One was Louis Rianer. But we didn't see her, my parents did. They dined with her at China Town. Another was Anna May Wong. All of us saw her. We had lunch with her at a Chinese restaurant.

She was slender and tall and pretty. We felt quite at home because she was after all Chinese. The boss of the restaurant wanted to take a picture of her but she refused, because he wanted to hang it on the wall.

Mother and Father saw quite enough of the stars. But we still wish to see some more.

House Hold

By Anor

In New York the first year we didn't have a maid. So we had to do the house hold work ourselfs. Mother manages the kitchen and Adet helped her. Every morning, that was when we don't go to school Adet took the dust cloth and the mob. I took the carpet-cleaner. Then we began to work at father's room because father's secatery was coming at nine thirty. Father helped us to clean the part near his desk. Because he admitted that under his desk it was dirty with matches and aches. After finishing that room we went in to the sitting room. Then mother's room, Adet's room, and our room. The thing we hate most was making the beds. The hardest to make were Meimei's and mine. So I often went into the kitchen to help mother dry the dishes and let poor Adet make our beds. We all liked to use the carpet-cleaner and disliked the mob. When the maid came to clean once a week we were always very glad to meet the day. But we all suffer from the smell of the amolnear except mother, who loved to smell it.

At about 11:00 Mother and Adet would go into the kitchen and cooked the lunch. Often the nice smell of the cooking made us go into the kitchen to eat something. The secetary loved to eat at our home. And she always felt hungry when she smelled the cooking as she typed. We had a call when we had things in hand to carry out the kitchen door, because the door could be opened both directions. We were afraid that two persons would come in the same door oppossit directions and spill the nice food. So we made an effort to say something when we were passing through that door the call was "hēo!" We all liked to shout it so that it had been a habit to say "hēo" when we were passing through that door. After lunch mother was always so tired. So Father helped wash the dishes. He did it very quickly. He often told us to time him. In five minutes he could wash and dry the dishes of five persons. Mr. Lin often broke dishes when he washed them. Mother was so afraid of the noise father made everytime.

Mother always told us to be careful of everything. But she couldn't tell father so. Father threw matches on the floor. Sometimes in the night father smokes without any light. Mother is always scared of catching fire.

Later we moved to a hotel and apartment. All we had to do was to cook and wash the dishes. Mother cooked, Adet helped. On washing the dishes, Adet was the one who washed most. I dry them about once a day. The whole family envied Meimei because she didn't have to do anything but sat and played. I hope some day we will all be Meimei.

First Time in a Subway and Elevated

By Adet

I AM glad to say that there isn't any subway or elevated in China. And some how we do get on time without rushing. After arriving at New York, Mr. and Mrs. Ts. took us all to have a ride in the subway. We have heard quite a lot about subway on our way to America and now we were really going to take a ride in it. Down the steps, through the corridor again down the steps, here we were going down to take a subway. The steps were dirty and the corrider had that sort of subway smell—bad air, gasolinish, etc. Then we reached the changing counter. Groups were waiting in line to get change. Mr. Ts. followed the line and the other waited. Anor and I looked at the automatic door which lets you pass when you drop a nickel. But the cracking of that turning thing sounded terrible to us as we weren't used to it. We saw men and women jumping down the steps, running through the corridor trying to catch the train. Their faces were awfully serious, mark my words!

Then the train arrived after a squeeking noise. Little came out and swamps got in. Five people went in without space for them. We sighed and wondered how the people in that car were going to feel. The door closed automatically. Some one came running down to rush the train but the door was closed already. With a shake and an uncomfortable noise it moved away.

Mr.Ts. finally got his change. He dropped the nickels one by one for us, in spite of the fact Anor liked to drop them. There was no time for her to drop as everybody was waiting at our back. We were in the platform waiting for train as everybody was. Meanwhile in waiting Mr. Ts. sloted many chewing gums for us. We chewed in the subway as a lot of them were chewing. It is a good idea to have these boxes on the iron pillars in the platform. A wonderful idea to use up left over penny for a piece to chew all day long. The train came and we got in. Mother told us to go ahead and push and so that was how we could get in.

The air was filthy, full of human breaths. We all held on a pole. The train swing and swang. I tried to look out the window; there were but some running black walls. We all didn't feel so fine except Mr. and Mrs. Ts. as they were used to it. I had a dread that I would have to take "subway" everyday.

Fortunately we got up the station after next and pushed out. Mrs. Ts. and I nearly didn't get out if there wasn't the man who pushed the door for us. He must have said in his heart, "These Chinese, they can't even take a subway." We were out the subway platform. Up the stairs and turned up the stairs and turned up, up and up we went. It was awful climbing, harder than a steep climb in the mountains. Hwee! we were out, out in the open air again. Thank god!

Later on we got used to the sound, smell and exercise of the subway and we didn't mind it. But anyway I prefer a bus on the surface of the earth.*

On 6th Ave. the 6th Ave. el was most disturbing when we crossed streets. We heard a sound of a truck and there wasn't any car. We all wondered; it was the elevated on top of us. First, we always wouldn't like to cross street when an elevated was runinng on top. There was a feeling that the crooked train on the rusty bars might fall any time. But ever since we were in New York we never heard of any incident of the elevated, except that heels were stuck between leaks.

I don't exactly remember when was the first time we took a el. But it was like this. The purpose was just to take a ride. Up the high steps we went. First very quickly then gradually slowed down. When we reached the top we were nearly out of breath. We all paused and then went in for change. The Elevated is never so crowdy as subway. It maybe because the el isn't fast enough. We didn't take the turning door for a new thing for we had seen those in the subway. Waiting on the platform it was rather cold. The people across the rails loked at us and we looked at them, face to face. The train came swiftly along. It stopped with the queerest sound, we all covered our ears, and we said we must be prepared for the next train. It wasn't the train we wanted and again we faced the opposite people. We leaned over to see if the train was

* *I was in the crowd and didn't enjoy it so much. I was like a mouse in a wood.—Meimei*

coming. It looked rather funny, like a black snake wiggling toward us.

It arrived and we stepped in. We could see the cars beneath from the leak between the wood board platform and the train. In the train it was less sutffy than in the subway. We looked out the windows there were the third floor rooms. Different things were seen: little dry plants on the firescapes; un-made beds; women cooking. They must be disturbed by the train or have got used to it.

At the turning point at 8th Ave. and 53rd Street the whole train swung. Anor nearly sat on somebody. We were frightened and at sixth Ave. & 53rd Street there was another swing, but we were prepared for it. So we all stood proudly straight as if we had taken elevated for a hundred times.

In front of Radio City we came out and down. The steps were just as hard to descend as to escend.

Promenade on Fifth Avenue one Afternoon

By Adet

If we had gone to movie on Saturday afternoon, we would spend the Sunday afternoon promenading on Fifth Ave. When we reached 49th Street we would turn right to the Canton Village and have supper there.

Well, we saw "Nothing Sacred" on Saturday of that weekend, and on Sunday we were on the fifth Ave. again. Our route that day was like this: the starting point was 64th St. & Central Park West, walking downtown up to 57th Street and then turning east. At fifth avenue we walked down town again. It was a clear day but a little windy. Mother had her white fur collar coat on, and the others all were pretty nicely dressed. Father and Anor walked about ten feet ahead of us. Sometimes he would turn back and wait for mother as she couldn't walk as quickly as father or the American girls. Then father and mother walked in line with us three ahead. Father smiled and spoke to mother about different things. Then in the middle of his speach he would turn to mother and tell her to look at the cute little legs of Meimei, and mother answered, "Anor looks nicer in American clothes than Adet." As there were few shops on Central Park West, we didn't look at them.

On 57th Street there are lots and lots of shoeshop. Mother looked at them one by one. Father said, "Come on, let's go in this one is nice." Mother said, "No, no, not this time." Father said, "Don't you like shoes?" Mother said, "Yes, but it is Sunday." We couldnt go in after all. Then father said he was hungry and he smiled and said, "I shall go in to the corner drug store and have a doughnut and coffee and I am sure when I come out I will still find you around this block. Anor come on." Anor went with father. When they came out we were but about eight shops ahead of them only, and Anor came saying she had ice cream. I didn't mind looking at the shops either, I didn't know why.

On fifth ave. there were a lot of well-dress mrs.s. walking striaght and quick. I didn't know whether I bumped into one lady or she bumped into me, but anyway when I wanted to say sorry she was gone already. As I looked back to see which one, another girl bumped into me again and I didn't have time to hear her say "sorry" either, if she ever said it. Diamonds looked nice on black velvet, and we guessed how many carets there are in that one and this one. On fifth ave. we not only looked at shops and also at people. "Look! she must have her face lifted." "She has orange powder on."

We reached fifth ave. church. Father said, "how about going in?" Mother answered, "Why, aren't you a pagan?" "Yes, of course, but I will go in for the music in spite of the preach." We went in. The choir was over so we sat for five minutes and then came out. On 49th St. we turned left and there was the neon light showing "Canton Village".

Mother at the Association

By Adet

SINCE the war started in China, the Chinese women do different works for China. In New York all the Chinese ladies started out an association for the relief of the refugees. Since there aren't many Chinese ladies in New York all of them came together and worked at it. Mother of course went into it too. She was the vice-chairman of the association. What they did every day was to send letter to rich ladies of New York and arrange diverse meetings and parties for the relief. In the office in 57th Street where they worked and laughed.

When the association was found mother had to go to the association almost every day besides her house hold. Sometimes she went there at 11 A.M. and had sandwich, coffee there and then came home at 4:30 P.M. It was of course pretty rushy for her, but nevertheless she enjoyed the working in the office. What mother did in the office was to write letters of thanks and put things into files and give suggestions on parties. She really worked hard. But in the office they talked a lot on this and that. Maybe Mrs. X. received a letter from Shanghai and she would tell the group about their metual friends. At lunch of course they rested a bit and there they joked and laughed. One of them might say, "Come on, work now." And then they worked again.

Mother enjoyed her hours in the association and there were of course arguements in it, but Mother never argued with them. While others were answering rather hot, she always kept quiet. I think it is rather wise to do that, but sometimes when others, more American-like, spoke very straight she ought to answer back, I think. Usually when mother came back from the office she always had a lot to tell us which we welcomed very much. It might be news of our Chinese friends in Shanghai or of the association members or the plan of the association.

Father was quite interested in the association plans and he often gave suggestions through mother. When we decided to leave America in February mother stopped going to the office for she had shopping, packing and lots of entertainment and engagements. Well the association still goes on, but I think without mother working there it is less enjoying and company.

Mother at the Association

By Anor

MOTHER went to the association everyday in New York. She finds it great fun. In the morning about

11:00 she goes there and have lunch there and comes back at about 5:00 or 6:00. She talked and laughed at the association, but in fact they often worked too.

Mother likes talkings and chatterings. She talked with Mrs. W. about their shoes and dress and everything what they find to talk. Miss S. is the nicest of all. She works and said, "work now, Mrses." But sometimes the things were too interesting to stop, and everybody joins. Miss S. has nuts and gums on the table. Once I went there she said, "That is one of the things we do in the office, Eat!" while she picked up a nut and put it into her mouth. I like to see her using the stamps. It was fun. She had a whole drawerful of stamps and full of colors. So when she opens the drawer the stamps will just pop out. I would like to sit there whole day and see her working. She smoked while she works. The best of all is to see her signing it was so quick and different from others. S. doesn't put powder on when she works. But it doesn't make her any more bad loking. People always say that she is the beautifulest girl in China and to me I think it is true.

Mrs. W. is the chairman of the association. She looks so skeelful. But so thin. Every time I saw her she looked thinner. Her dresses are espacially beautiful and artestic. She was the one who talks with mother most. She is a nice woman, and funny too. She likes mother so much.

There are many others that I don't know so well.

Mother is the one I know best among the association. Mother works quickly and talks very much. She liked the association so much that even when she knows there was nothing to do she would drop in and gabble with anyone there. Mother ate her lunch at 2:00. I always get hungry before time. Mother would said to me that they have their lunch at 2:00. But I don't think how they can bear it so long. But mother could. She worked and talked and smoked in the association that she could forget the hunger. But if I were Mother I certainly couldn't bear the hunger. But maybe I could finish the boxful of nuts on S's table.

New York Theatres

By Anor

ONE day in November. We were going to see a movie. Father had gone to a lunch with someone. Before going out Father said, "Let's go to Music Hall at 2:30 this afternoon. We will meet at the Radio City first floor. At the book shop." When the time has come we were all at the book shop, looking through the window to see if they have Father's books on the window. Then we all went in. There was a great big crowd in line to get in the theatre. Adet suggested that we won't have to wait if we go down, there is another entrance. So we went down and we were so happy to find it true. We had to stand in line inside. We had to wait about an hour. Finally we got in. The ushers led us to the sits. Mother is always with Meimei. They often took one set. Adet hates to be seperated with us and sit alone. But when it is crowded she has to. It is better to be alone than to stay at home. When it was a recess time we always looked around to see who is in which section.

The first night that I came out in New York my impression was, there are so many theatres in New

York and that in front of the theatres they use so many lights. The first theatre I went in was Roxy's. We went there because we stayed in the same block, Hotel Taft. I was disappointed when we went in the Capital Theatre because I didn't see any stage-show in the theatre. But later we didn't see as much stage-show as we did at first.

The theatre we often go in is Music Hall. We liked the picture every time we went in, but one. The reason we go to Roxy quite often is because of Shirley Temple. Sometimes when we would want a change we would go to the small theatres on Broadway. Mother likes Music Hall is because the chairs are comfortible. Father, I don't think, has any choice. Adet likes it is because the pictures are good. I too is the same reason. Meimei follows every where mother goes.

It is a great experience to see the New York theatres. I will never forget the stage-show in New York City.

I Catch the Bus Going to School

By Anor

EVERYDAY I get up at 7:00. The curtains were so dark. But I have to get up in the middle of a deep sleep. Tic tac tic tac struck the clock. I got to run to the clock, oh, quarter of seven. So I pulled the curtains up. The pegions were at the windows waiting for food. But they will have to wait till to-morrow. I don't have time now. I pulled out the drawers and take out all the things I need. I went to the kitchen and the milk was still at the door, so I rushed to the door, there it was, with the newspapers. I took it in. But when I got to the kitchen, the toast was already black and burned. The room was full of smoke. There, I was wasting two pieces of bread. All right, I don't want toast. So I took out another piece and didn't toast it. But oh, the paper cork was so tight! Pop! The milk was spilled. Lucky, it spilled just a little. After five minutes I finished. But I forgot my orange. It's all right, I can go without it. "Anor! go and get the letters." But I didn't have much time. I gallopped down stairs, as the elivater was always too slow. "Any letters?" "Yes." Oh! it was a letter from Amoy! Mother would be so happy. "Ma, a letter from your home." Mother jumped out of bed and read the letter. "Zooooo" Father snored. Mother pulled the curtains. "Snow!" I shouted. Mother read it quickly. "What did it say?" I asked. Mother told me to lower my voice. Father was sleeping "Zooor Whoooo!" I laughed in my stomach. Oh. It was late, I forgot all about school. Mother told me to go slowly and said my clock was wrong. "May I phone?" ME 7—1212. "When you hear the signal the time will be seven fifty-six and three quarters." Oh! late. I put my coat on and went running down. "Good-bye!" I yelled. "I could see that you are late by not saying 'Good morning' to me" said the man selling the papers. I smiled to him and I went flying across to the bus stand. Well, the bus just went. Why didn't hurry down 5 seconds earlier to get the bus? Another five minutes was gone and no bus. I saw a huge thing, it must be the bus, but it was a truck. Well, finally it did come. "Oh hello N—— it is so late." "No" she said. We came to school. But the school was not opened yet. "Oh, after all the rushings" I said, "The school is not opened. The clock must be wrong."

Going to School with Meimei

By Anor

MEIMEI is a very slow girl at dressing. I am not too fast at it, but is not as slow as she is. In the morning I was the one to call Meimei up sometimes. It happened that her class started at 10:10 and mine at 8:30. So there was a great difference between the two. I said it was late and Meimei said it was early. When I finished my breakfast Meimei hadn't finishd washing her face yet. I had to make breakfast for her because she was "small" which I hated to do. I even had time to play for a while while I was waiting for Meimei. "Hurry up!" I kept on yelling to her. But she was the slowest girl in eating. A mouthful of bread would take her about ten minutes to chew and swallow down and the matter is, the more you hurry her the slower she eats. So the only way was just to let her alone. Poor Meimei, when she got to school she was the earliest among all her classmates who came after 9:00.

When I went to a trip and came back later than usual, Oh gosh! she would cry. Cry till the doorman, her teacher and some parents of the school help her to telephone home and tell father to come to fetch her for lunch.

"Ho, Ho, your sister cried. You ought to see how cute she was." said the school doorman. Meimei was always so sad when she cried. But a nice sister would take out a handkerchief and wipe her tears. It happened that I am NOT that kind of sister. All I could do was laugh. I knew it was rude of me. But not my fault, I couldn't help it. If we had a festival and reherse later then usual I had to come out with my custume and tell her not to worry about me. But indeed she was quite nice at school. Seldom cries but you know all the fuss she makes when she does. My friends like her very much. She said "Yes" or "No" when I was with her but when I was not there she would make a speech. She really didn't course me much trouble but one thing I hate most was when she was sick or anything. I had to go to her classroom and tell the teacher. One more thing was when her teeth was black the nurse came and asked me "WHY?"

[*And poor Anor she had to tell all about my awful black teeth but what can I do if my teeth are like that. —Meimei*]

My Impression About the American Children

By Anor

THE first day I went to the American school everyone loked at me with wonder. "How can a Chinese girl get in the same class with us?" I suppose were in my classmates' minds. "How can I speak English fast enough to hear a word that they say?" this sentence was in my mind. I still remember the first lesson. It was about "' ". Everyone write a phrase like "boy's shoes" to use the appastufre. I was glad to find them learning the thing I learnt in third grade. At ressest a mop came and looked at me queerly. As if I were a strange animal sitting on a chair! Some one try to speak with me and through I didn't know a word of English. Surprised to find me answering their questions. Whispers about me were a lot that day. But I didn't care.

"Teach me how to speak Chinese" was asked for many times without my astonishment. What came in my mind most was their slang, Slang slang and slang. I couldn't bear them "half, calf, can't, etc." were all differently pronounced. A girl came to me and said, "You are the only one in the class that speaks good English." I didn't know what it mean for my English was poor. At last I knew she meant I didn't speak their slang.

Americans to me are all very different from my Chinese friends. So quick and straight forward. If any one borrowed a pencil from me and I said no, it would make her think I am no friend of her. So everytime "yes" was my answer. And by my behaving they became fond of me after the first year. One would fight for things while I laugh at them. So I think they tried to behave better to make good impression for me to tell to my Chinese friends. There are good and bad things about them which I hope they wouldn't be hurt if I say so. I will say their good first.

They are, well I can't find the word, anyway they are keen on doing a new thing, love animals and love sport. Good at memerizing and work together. Love punctuality, and love freedom.

About the weakness I am going to say just what I think. Really I can't find anything to say but there are, I am sure. Oh yes. The girls talk about love afairs too early as I think. They tease each other too much. Don't think for others. And think they live in the best of all countries. And are sophomoric I will stop here for I don't want them to feel that I am bossy and critical.

Sport in School

By Anor

I AM not like the American children. I mean the way they play with balls. I can't feel like playing, for the way they play scares me.

First of all I have no interest in playing any kind of gymnastic games. Even in China, they play very softly, I am afraid of it. Those games to me are nothing but running and catching balls and sometimes falling and sometimes the ball hits you. I don't take sport as an important thing in school. So, when I don't know how to play, or people laugh at me, I just don't care to learn and pay no attention to it. At the hour of sports, all I know what to do is to change into the shoes, be ready to be laughed at, and stand at where they tell me to stand.

The way they kick the ball just make me feel as if that the ball will drop on my head. So I avoid it. And after seeing where the ball dropped it made me laugh at myself. And then when it really happened that I could have caught the ball and I didn't the girls would say,

"Oh, Anor, Anor, Oh——", which made me sick and whenever it was their turn to miss the ball she'd keep quiet. But I never shout at people for I know myself that I can do no better.

I don't care to learn any new games, but if I do I care not to make any improvement. So all that the word "gymnastic" means to me is "a thing that I don't care."

I don't mind if I don't go to that class at all.

In China I am bad also at this kind of things. I had to run with them and I felt awkward.

So at last I supopse I have to say that running is not for me.

The Maids Stella and Nancy

By Anor

STELLA is a color maid introduced by our landlady. She was quite black enough to scare us when we just came from China, as there were no black men in China. Every Tuesday she came to wash and every Saturday she came to clean the house.

Mother always coked something special for us each Tuesday, nicer food and bigger portions. We asked her why. "Because the maid Stella is coming today." Mother is always so good and kind to servants. "Oh, I don't like no more American food, madame. The China food is so delicious." But when mother cooked American food she ate just the same. Stella was often late, when the bell rung, there she was "Madame my daughter married yesterday. About sixty people came, and I got drunk." Mother could only excuse her. But we don't. Nobody but mother could stand the smell of her. It smelled like the washing soap cooked with some onions. And when Saturday came, we all hated the day. Stella came with "amonia" (a kind of cleaning lotion). Oh when the Amonia was used in this room, nobody could step in to the room even when we passed through the door we had to hold breathing for a minute. After she had gone, the smell was gone. Stella didn't clean for us later when we moved to a hotel.

But she did the washing. The laundry came in a big basket. When we took out the dresses one by one, the smell would just the same come out, and when the basket of laundry was taken out, the room would have the smell of her just the same.

When we got to the hotel, Thank goodness, the maid that came to clean everyday in the hotel was a nice woman named Nancy. Nancys are always nice.

She was a prudent girl. Once she broke Father's "Clay horse" and she was so scared and reproached all the week. Mother was so nice to her. She gave her a box that grandfather gave mother when mother married. She chattered with her as she was cleaning the rooms. Nancy told mother surreptitiously about how she broke the engagement and how she and her mother-in-law fought and all sorts of things.

She was the maid I liked best among all the maids we ever used.

Shopping at Macy's

By Anor

Mo. Y.T. Look, you have burned your coat.

Fa. Well!

Mo. Come with us, I am bringing the children to Macy's to buy something.

F. No I don't need anything.

M. Yes Y.T. look at your coat. You need a new one. Come on.

F. No, I am all right. Who is better dressed than I am?

M. Dick.

F. No. I don't want shopping.

M. Please Y.T. You need many things, necktie, socks, shirt, shoes, etc.

F. Please, you know I don't like shopping.

M. Come on, Adet.

F. Maybe I am going too.

M. Good! Good Y. T.!

We arrived at Macy's

M. Adet, take out the lest.

Ad. Toothbrush, Bon ami, soap, shoes, Meimei's dress, etc.

M. I think we better go down to the basement first.

F. I am going to the book dept.

M. Find us at the children's dept.

F. O. K.

At the children's dept.

F. Oh gosh!

M. What?

F. This, matches.

M. Ha ha. I am so sorry.

F. Parden me sir, have you got a match.

M. Y.T. Don't go hunting for matches. That's one thing I don't like about shopping with you.

F. A-sap! (a name of Meimei's, it is a milk name) so lucky, what a pretty dress.

M. Who choose it? Your wife did.

F. No I did.

M. You weren't here when I choose it.

F. Well!

M. Well?

F. Come, have you gotten through? I am HUNGRY!

M. What!

F. HUNGRY!

M. How much is this one?

Sellsgirl. $3.99.

M. Y.T. here's the money. Give it to her.

F. I have my money.

M. No, I want you to give it to her. Anor, pass it to Y.T.

F. Why? I have my money.

M. But I bought the dress.

F. Then why don't you give it to her?

M. No, you.

F. Here. Hong, finished?

M. No, I am not half finished.

F. Good lord. Who wants to go with me to the TOY dept.?

M. Oh, but Y.T. aren't you going to buy your coat?

F. No, come on Anor. We will go home first.

M. Then what is the use of you coming to Macy?

F. Books.

My First Experience in Acting

By Anor

SINCE the war broke out, Mother goes to an association to help China. They thought of giving a play for China. There was a woman named C——. She taught me how to act in the play.

It was a tireing thing, every week twice. It disturbed my studying. She taught me to sing the conversation. I had to do it loud. The first few times there were many people around me. It made me so afraid to meet the day.* Later when I got used to it it was all right. C—— said that I must put one hand in front and one hand in back when I walk and then change around. I had to pratice every day at home. Then when I learned it I had to learn to bow at her. How I should do with my fingers and how long should I do it. Every time she started for acting she would drink a cup of *hot* water to ease her throat. Then in the middle of the thing she would stop and repeat then start all over again, then she would stop and talk to me and then start again. She did it for many times. But some how we got finished with the three hours. There was a man to play the music. The thing was so sharp that it hurts the ear.

Mother hunted for the custome for a long time. When I try it on, I don't look like me any more. I was a prince. My hair was all hidden in my crown. The thing was orange, as long as possible. It almost made me fall. C—— was so busy at her own custome that she didn't see me wearing mine until the day of the play.

Mother was inviting as many people as possible, whereas I was wishing for nobody to come. Meimei was in the thing too. But she didn't have to say a word.

Somehow I learned the play all right. Then the day came.

In the morning mother, Meimei and I went for a

* *I was so nervous.—Meimei*

dress rehercal, from 10:00 to 12:00. When we huried home for lunch.

Right after lunch we went to the Hotel again. We rushed just like Americans. There sat C—— and a maid in the dressing rom. What I call dressing room is just a part taken from the room and use a screen to part. C—— was a real actress. I was a temporary one. C—— sat on a stool with a comb on one hand and a brush on the other. Some peices of hair were put on C——'s head. It took her thre hour's to dress. The guests poured in more than I wished. But as the matter of fact I wished for *none*. There were smoke all over the room. In a short while all were ready for the play. Out came C——, Meimi and me. The music began. My hands were cold. Father was looking at me and I was scared like a mouse. C—— began her singing, and Meimei and I looked at each other with fear. C——'s singing stopped. I sang without my mind. Then the walk came. I went just as C—— told me, but not so good. I stood with my large crown that covered my face aside. Mother said I had to put rouge on to let people in back see me. But I said I didn't care if they don't. Soon, in this way or that the thing was finished. Out we came again to bow and grin. After that I took all the useless dress out, and I was me again. I went out with my *own* dress. Thus I feel I am just like the other people.

A Visit to Coney Island

By Anor

In China we heard so much Coney Island and now we were going to Coney Island. We took a subway and in it we sat for two hours. After we got there there was a good crowd standing in front of a certain house. We got in and walked around. Father and Meimei and I went to sit on the cars that ran so fast that made my stomach empty. Up and down we went. Mother and Adet were afraid to bump into something so they didn't come with us. We three went in the seats of two persons because no one wanted to sit alone. It was a nice ride. Then the whole family went in to a dark, dark place. Father lead the family with one hand holding Meimei's hand. Adet and Mother and I walked closely together. It was a long distance, but we went and thought we were going out. But a man came and said, "Let's take the elevater." I knew it was not a regular elevater because no one would invite me to take it for fun. The man told father "Hold her tight" and we three were in one car. "Hold her tight" certainly sounded dreadful. I knew something strange would come out of the car. The bell rung and off we went to the magic carpet. The sort of carpet went up and down so quick that one would fall down. Father, Meimei and I lay all the way down. There there was a place to let us slide down. Thus we were out. We stood there to wait for mother and Adet. I thought to myself, "Poor them. They are going to have a nice and smooth ride." The bell rung again and out came Mother and Adet. Adet, as the usual way, laughed all the way out.

There are many other things that we went on, such as riding in a car that each drived his own. In it Father lost a one dollar bill. And a boat that went up very high and came tumbling down into a river. Any way that was Coney Island. Father and I was the most adventurus. Mother and Adet did go on much nice trips, but just the same Adet laughed on everything she went on for NO reason. Meimei was quiet all the way going and coming back. But everyone enjoyed it very much.

In Atlantic City

By Anor

F. What do you think of going to Atlantic City?
M. All right.

Thus we start packing and in a while we were ready. It was spring vacation. We went to the station. Mother bought some lemon drops for us while father bought the tickets.

We arrived in Atlantic City! We hired a car and told the driver to take us to a not too bad or swell hotel. Well, we stayed in a common hotel with everything we wanted and the next morning we started out to explore the city. We went to the silver tower, I think was the name, and went in a movie. Then we walked on the boardwalk and there down on the sand were those artists. Mother gave him permission to draw Meimei and I, but the conclution was that Meimei and I looked like twins. So after we were out of his sight, out went the two pictures into the sea. We went to a five and ten cent store for fun as we often did. When entering the store, we had no idea whatsoever to buy anything but to look in. But when we exited each one had a package in his hand. That is the trouble with those 5 and 10¢ stores. We think this is cheap and that is cheap so we buy them and then the total of little things of 5 and 10¢ make a lot.

The most interesting is the silhouette. We each stood before him and he used a pair of siccors and cut our shape which was the most wonderful thing. Each one looked like us. Then we went to ride on the donkey. I enjoyed it with fear for I am very easy to be afraid. We took a picture with us on the donkeys which looked very queer.

I think we are so funny people. We don't go to see a city as it should be seen but go and do the things which should be done in other places. We went into a movie and saw "Maytime" there when we heard that it was Jeanette McDonald. But movies are not the thing that's important in Atlantic City. And as you know, we went into a 5 and 10¢ store as if there weren't any in New York! But anyway we do what ever we like and enjoyed more.

Anagrams in Havana

By Adet

"How 'bout a game of Anagrams?" was always the question after lunch or dinner in Havana. The answer was "o.k., good," and then we started the game.

In Havana, Cuba, we stayed for a month one summer. Mrs. Ts. and Mr. Ts. lived with us in a cute one flat house that had a big verandah in front. Mr. and Mrs. Ts. are very familiar with us as we know her since Mrs. was a girl. In fact she is our relative. Havana would be quite hot, if there wasn't the cooling sea breeze. We usually wore one piece only and Father had his comfortable pajamas-like Chinese clothes on. The house was not so cool in the mornings and afternoons we generally spent our time in the wide verandah, where comfortable sedan chairs were provided. In the morning we generally read news paper (as that was the time when the war started) or novels. It was quite wonderful that I did a summary of Chinese history in these lazy mornings. Soon came lunch. It was always a good and hearty meal. Then we relaxed to the verandah again. We had pineapple or melons for deserts. There the men and Meimei would prepare things for the game while the ladies went in and washed and combed themselves. Meimei was always enthusiastic about Anagrams though she just sat at the back of mother's chair during the game. Once in a while mother would tell her to draw checkers for her and if it was a good one each group would ask her to draw for them. Meimei put her concentration on the game and she would whisper to mother to get a "gift" or "boy" or "her" while mother was thinking for harder words and forgetting the easy ones. Mother's group would thank Meimei for it, but the other groups would say, "Meimei, don't be too clever and don't tell mother the word." Meimei understood this was sort of a compliment and she smiled. Anor was most excited by this game. Often we two formed a group and when she saw something that other don't see she would pinch me hard and could not control her laughter. Well, then others saw her laughing and they concentrate more and finally they got the word. I always told her to stop laughing, but she couldn't help it. Father often took the game quite seriously and so did Mr. Ts.

When we played we often divided into three or four groups. Group one Mother and Anor and sometimes Meimei, Group two Young Mrs. Ts. and I; group (3) Mr. Ts.; Group 4. Father and sometimes with Meimei. This was always the groups but we switched around. Sometimes Meimei didn't want to play and she did her (for grown-ups) jig-saw puzzle alone. I don't know why we were so pleased with this game. We almost did it after every lunch and dinner except we were invited out. We all dreaded an ordinary friend coming in the middle of the game and we should have to break up. We often played until all the covered alphebets were turned and counted how many we had. The winner was not certain. As luck counted a great deal. The ends of the games were always the most exciting. Each one stood up one by one and Father and Mother often walked over to other's side and looked. These games were always very cheerful and humorous. There were always jokes and stories of old-time friends told, when we weren't taking the game eagerly. And also I must mention there were always tea and candies during the game, and the tea pot was often refilled. Since we played it so often there were things like these come out. "If" changes into "fig" again to "gift". They were cleverly thought out by different people and used into a habit. Another one is "my" into "may" into "many". So whenever we saw "may" we thought of the whole lot.

The game ended up when we left Havana. In New York we also played sometimes but not so frequently as everybody was busy.

What They Ask Me About China

By Anor

In the West people ask very silly questions about China. These are the questions they asked me.

1. Do you have chairs in China?
2. Do you have tables in China?
3. Do you eat opium?
4. Do you get colds in China?
5. You eat with drumsticks, don't you?
6. You eat pigeon nests just like that don't you?
7. Why don't you have small feet?
8. Why aren't your eyes two ends up?
9. Are there cars in China?
10. Don't you have a pigtail on your back?
11. Don't you wear a bowl shaped upside down hat?
12. You were pajamas on the street, don't you?

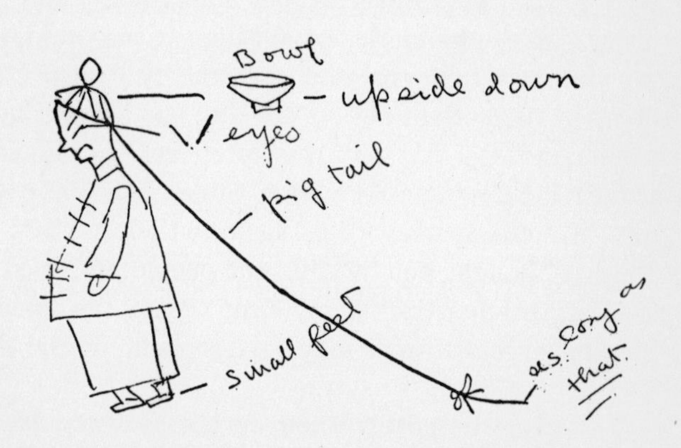

WHAT THEY ASK ME ABOUT CHINA

There are many of these questions but these are enough for any one to see what the Western children think of China.

Sometimes they hurt our feelings to think of what they think of China. Those questions are just silly, that's all. And I wonder how they dare to ask. It seems to me that they take these Chinese not as human beings but just as something strange and curious to know.

I think if they go to China they will see what China is really like. They will be supprised.

The answers to all those questions are:

1. Chairs in China? Yes
2. Tables in China? Yes
3. Eat Opium? No
4. Get Colds? Yes
5. Eat with Drumsticks? No
6. Eat pigeon nests like that? No
7. Have small feet? No
8. \ / eyes? No
9. Cars in China? Yes
10. Pigtails? No
11. An upside down bowl hat? No
12. Pajamas on the St.? No

So you see the answers are just the same as an American would answer those questions about America.

I wish all those who have the old fashion ideas about China mixed with Japan would get rid of those ideas.

Do I Like New York?

By Anor

If they don't mind I'd say I like Paris better. But sometimes I do long for New York. It is real hard to say.

First, it is no fun at all walking in New York streets, except seeing shop windows.

It's very convenient to travel in New York.
I like Dogs when they are Hot in America.
I like American schools.
The people walk much too quick in the streets.
I hate their lunches.
I love thier buses.
I have no openion about the Negros.
I don't like their elevaters.
I dislike skyscrapers.

I like the bottom of Radio City.
I like the movies in New York.
I think the slang is awful.
I don't like the American pronunciation.
Trees are no where to be seen but in the parks.
I like to see sandwich men.
I like the cafeteria.
I like their ice cream.
I don't like the way they say "China Town".
I don't like what they think of China.
I like to see Broadway at night.
I like the lights going round the theatres.
I think the flash lights are awful, so I close my eyes and make them small when ever they take a flash light picture of me. So I never look nice in those flash lights.
No fun shopping at New York.
No beauties in New York.
A heavy skin of dust in New York.
They rush just when they have nothing to do.

Now, the only thing I care very much to see again in New York is the stage show in Radio City.

Any show in Paris is no comparison to it.

Alas! New York has it good and bad sorted out.

Part III. EUROPE

On S.S. Conte de Savoia

By Anor

On the boat there were two teams for eating. One was for eating "Roast Beef" the other is "Green Vegetable" team. Of course Father was the leader of "Roast Beef" teem. Almost every meal on board the ship when there was Roast Beef Father ate it. After three or four days the waiter knew it already. When there was Roast Beef the waiter would immediately run to father when father stepped into the dinning room and tell him, "There is roast beef on the menu." Father laughed at that but was not ashamed of it. About the "Green Vegetable" team. The leader was Mother. Every meal mother ordered Vegetable and added a "green" on top of the word "Vegetable".

As to the members of the teams it was not always the same members. But the leaders were always the same.

Adet some times liked the beef but sometimes vegetables. When Anor and Meimei wanted beef, Adet often accompanied mother to eat vegetables or any dish mother had.

Anor was often on the "Roast Beef" team. Because she liked it better. But when the chicken or any thing which mother took was better then beef, Anor often regraded but ate the beef for father.

Meimei was often droven into the "Green Vegetable's" team. But she was often in between. Both teams wanted her because she was the smallest in the family.

Father and Mother always laughed at each other. Father thought Mother ate too much vegetables and Mother thought Father won't do without beef.

Inside Vesuvius

By Adet

AH, Vesuvius, the living volcano, and we went in.

The day after we arrived Naples what we were going to see were to be Vesuvius and Pompeii. Our impressions on Pompeii was almost overwhelmed by that of Vesuvius. That noon we had food at the foot of Mount V. and after that we took the taxi going up the mountain. It was country road at first only, but from the window one saw the snow covered giant in front. At that time we weren't so sure about going up there, because we were afraid that while looking down into a big hole with materials boiling one might slip down. But we were going to ask a guide about it. When we reached about 1/5 the height of the mountain, there was a small house with several red faced guides. While father was informing we were sitting in the car covered with blankets and all. Funny that we all felt adventurous at the same time. "Go" we all said and we went. In our hearts there were something itchy wondering what it would be like. Mother had her protection of this danger that we five were there if the lava flow out, we all perish, not just a few. While we were discussing all sorts of thing "if happen", we came to the roadend where the car couldn't go any more. Up or not, this was another hesitation, but up was the decision. In the heavy fog mother was helped by the guide walking in front and back in the thick mist. Anor and I, Father and Meimei, hands in hands. It was raining a bit and rather cold. Father put the blanket around Meimei to make her a little Indian child. Anor was holding my hand all the time and she said she preferred to walk inside, than outside and she got her preference.

IN THE VESUVIUS CRATER

Well, you know, one gives in as a sister. Some places we seperated for there wasn't space for two. We went Zig zag up the mountain and were eating bits of pure white snow from the roadside.* Mother was quite in front usually and we shouted, "Yo-ho," back and forth in order to get in touch with each other. On the way father asked a question: what would you do if the lava flow down suddenly? We all agreed it is best to roll straight down mountain with our heavy coat protecting

* *And we ate glaces also.—Meimei*

our body. The guide told a lie about reaching the top in twenty minutes. I don't know how long it took us, but it was long.

We came to a place suddenly when one heard a roar of the sea each three minutes. It was the roar of lava turning inside the heart of Vesuvius. Later when we thought of the roars we were frightened, but I was not afraid while hearing the real sound. I guess I just didn't know the danger, that's all.

Then we reached the crator mouth and it wasn't a deep hole as we imagined but a stretching ground of hardened lava. The lava hardened as it was flowing down. There we were walking on hot lava twenty days ago and it was still warm despite the cold mountain wind. The rolls of lava crawling down and across were like thick black ropes 8 inches in diameter. Some like wiggling snakes. Each of us had a guide except father, and Meimei was carried on the shoulder of a strong man. She was the most comfortable one I think. The road was bumpy enough and in addition the guides dragged us along literally. But that was a good way, I must admit, otherwise we won't have this thrill at all. We were dragged along about quarter of an hour before we were let loose, twenty feet from the mouth of lava coming out. The lava went up about one or two feet and then flowed down in big rolls. It was red hot and the roars were loud in the next peak. Freightened we were a bit. Father stepped a few steps forward and mother hurrily called him to retreat. Two guides used a poker and got a piece of hot lava from the crack and put a coin in it to give it as souvenir.

In many places there were leaks or cracks and we had to walk across it, of course the cracks weren't big, but big enough to see the red hot lava underneath. Some spots there were thin layers of soufa and the smell steamed up to our noses which made our breath uncomfortable. At the same time there was steam coming out from the cracks in all places. At such a time, we all felt strange; Meimei sat quietly on the shoulders of the guide and didn't know what to do at all. I felt as if in another planet, where there was no tree or living plants, we the only explorers arrived there and could no more go back to the earth, for there seemed no road back. What made we feel so far from the earth must be the shapes of harden lava we were stepping on, so unimaginable! We have all forgotten the snow on the way up, the sunny plains below, and the blue sea ahead. In addition the horrible roars were booming out inside the mountain about 40 feet from us. According to what they said the roads and surfaces changed all the time, maybe the road we took before is now again covered with a new layer of lava. It changed according to the ways of the wind. Perhaps one day it might flow down the mountain once more, since the surface is accumulating more and more.

Coming down seemed more easy and much quicker. We took leaps and jumps on the rough, uneven lava. We fell or knealed down once or twice, but were immediately dragged up by the strong arms of the guide. I didn't have time to think whether I did hurt myself or not, for my mind was so occupied in searching a evener place to put my feet on before the guide dragged me too far. Later on mother was almost lifted by the two guides. Her feet, she said, merely tapped on the ground. At that time nobody had time to think of anything but her own walking. The guides were told several times to slow down by father and they said yes, but went on the same.

When we were all out of the crater we were so happy. Though we still couldn't see the world through the thick clouds but at least we could roll down in case the lava overflow. We walked down and met snow. We still picked clean snow for our mouth. In a short time we were down at the car. It was about 5 o'clock. On our way we saw a man and a woman with heels three inches high starting their way up. The woman seemed already rather helpless; I don't believe they will go into the crater. In the car we counted our loses. Five pairs of shoes were roughened on the heels and the points.* Mother and I got a cut on the feet which we were quite proud of, and of course the two pairs of stockings were included.

When we got to the hotel we all took a bath and had a hearty meal and went to bed with our minds occupied in thinking the great experience of a lifetime we took that after noon. Days later we still kept on discussing the danger we took, the sight we saw, the sound we heard in entering the Mount Vesuvius.

* *But not mine. I am still wearing this pair of shoes. —Meimei*

Florence

By Anor

We went through Italy and passed Naples, Rome, and Florence. I like Florence best, and so do all of us.

The Italians are fat, hearty, and not so very clean.

The hotel we stayed in had a severe manager. I

broke a piece of china, and was so scared that I had to run to the toilet while father was telling him, for I thought he might run after me. But later he made us pay for it.

Italy has many cats, especially at hotels. We stayed in three hotels, and they all had cats, that didn't suit me very much as I am dead scared of cats.

In the morning we walked about a little distance where the Arno River is. It was a very peaceful river, with many bridges over it, some with houses and shops and some just plain. Some with a great smell and some very nice. Along the river are shops and hotels, all for travellers for they are all expensive. Mother bought a set of coral for herself and it was extremely beautiful. We bought leather boxes with our names engraved on them. But father lost one as he was having doughnuts in a shop. Those were very delicious, with chocolate cream in them.

We hired a carriage one day, and found the driver can say, "I, er, san, see, woo, liun, shi, pa, gion, she," which is one to ten in Chinese. We drove to the Cathedral. According to them, it was the most rich and beautiful Cathedral in the world. We paid to get in. But Meimei and I found the Cathedral most unpleasant. For it was *not* a place where people prayed, but just a room about as large as the 6 P class room of the Ethical Culture school. Of course it is rich, furnished with marble all over. But worst of all, is that the walls is surrounded with tombs, yes, tombs all sticking out of the wall. Father dared to touch them, but Meimei and I were not one bit interested.

We also went to the market, it was wet and dirty,

we saw people eating right at the market the stomach of a cow, raw.

Adet bought Vergin Mary's poslane model. It was father's gift to her for she liked it *so so* much.

We liked Florence because it was just right, Naples was too quiet, Rome too noisy, and Florence was just right.

We lived near a college where students were, in our hotel there were 5 or 6 students. They played American jezz music. Danced "jezz dance" and they were all like Americans except one. Who, as father said, was the cleverest, for he sat quietly down and listened.

We stayed five days in Florence, and enjoyed it very much.

The First Night in Nice

By Adet

It was about ten at night; every body was dozing in the train except Anor and Mother. I was called for the dream land and threw on my coat in a half sleepy way. We rushed down the train and called the porters immediately for we had ten pieces of luagage. It was fortunate that the train stopped for ten minuets in Nice, otherwise we might be carried away to Cannes or father away.*

We put all our things in the hotel service bus and the driver took us to the hotel which we reserved. I

* *We nearly were carried away for three of us were nearly asleep. If we didn't have Anor we were carried away. Anor quickly said, "Nice," so we all jumped up. —Meimei*

was all awaked again and so were the others; we looked out to see the lights of Nice in dark. The promenade with shinning lamps looked very lovely. We drove a little way up the hill and there was the hotel looking nice and neat. We all were quite pleased with the sight of it, and we thought we were quite luckily to get this nice hotel in this crowded carnival season. A nice middle aged ladies receive us. Father used his newly-learned French to say that we had reserved two rooms from the Thomas Cook in Florene. The little French lady was quite surprised to find us here. She said something very quickly in French to father which meaned that she thought we reserved two rooms for March 23 and this was Febuary 23, she hadn't got a room except in the cellar. She was sorry and very sorry. We visited the rooms in the cellar. They were not so good and we didn't like the idea of sleeping in "cellar". Well, we bid good-bye and the driver drove us down the hill. It was very hard to find a room in the hotels in those carnival Days. The bus-driver looked into different little pemphets and he told father that he was bringing us to Pension Villa Bella. We were satisfied, and mother wanted to get to the hotel for Meimei was a bit sleepy.

On the grand boulevard facing the sea was the Pension Villa Bella placed. It was pretty grand and swank from the outside. We stepped in. A young madamoselle in black with a little white fur collar received us. Then a man in butler suit with glasses on the middle of his nose and a strong man with a cheap suit came. Father said, "We like to have two rooms with bath, do you have them and how much if you please." The three gathered in a group and whispered and argued in a lower voice. We were surprised to see a hotel hostess and managers talked this way. They told father the price. It was a bit dear but father said it is quite all right for a night. Then the man in butler suit said to father, "Are you Chinese?" He answered calmly, "Yes." Then he suddenly spoke Chinese hallo to us in very bad Chinese. We were surprised to see him speak Chinese. Then he asked Meimei how old is she in Chinese. Before she answered the other man told him to

THE DANCING WAITER AT NICE

get the baggage and he went. Then the lady said they would only give us one room with bath, because there are few rooms. Well, since it is just for a night it is o.k. We went up the room. It was very big and the furniture were good, but old. The carpet looked quite expensive but it was stained with ink and there were little holes eaten by worms. The bath room was very old fashioned too. We told them to put two more beds in as there were room for them. All the three of them brought up the baggages adding a maid. The man who spoke Chinese to us talked to father again. He said he was in Peking eighteen years ago. But in his funny

Peking dialects there were Amoy (our home town) and Canton dialect in it. He seemed quite misterious. He said he was working the Chinese counsulate. He was now the friend of the owner of the hotel—the healthy-looking man in a farmer-like suit.

We got ready for a little supper and went down the stairs. Mother didn't feel very at home as in the other hotels. We sat down the table and all three of them came. The hotel owner apologized for not having a regular waiter at this time of the night. The young lady came and went and the other man stood by father and talked to him. The kitchen boy came with cold ham. He had a striped vast on and a bright yellow and black tie. His face and hands were extremely red. I do not know why. He had quite a pile of dishes in his hands. He skipped to the right side of mother and curtsied and them jumped a little jump and knocked with the folk on the plate three times and then put the plate down. He curtsied again and then skipped to the right side of me and did the same ceremony. It was cute to all of us and we couldn't control our laughter. But soon we felt dizzy from looking at his moments. Mother couldn't stand it she was very nevious. And he gave us napkins, he put his thumb into his mouth first and then despatched the napkins. We all felt not so good. The queer man with glasses stood besides us and talked to father in Chinese and he said he knew 8 thousand words and he wrote hastily with his finger on the table cloth. We were quite amazed. Every thing was so queer and misterious here. The owner came from middle Frence and the lady was born in Madagaska (a island off Africa). The carpet in the dining room worth a million francs and the bathrooms are so bad. Everything was so immutual as a hotel, as a manager, and as a waiter. We could excuse them of the ham for dinner, for the time was quite late. But the whole management was awfully, and the people were all misterious. We all presumed that the owner must be a farmer in Middle France and he came to Monte Carlo and won a lot of money, and then he bought this villa and turned it into a hotel. The friend must be a friend who helped everything. But we could not solve the lady from Madagaska. We saw the owner calling his "friend" to bring in the bread and fruits and do different things. Mother couldn't stand the whole situation expecially the dancing waiter. She didn't have coffee and went up to the room with Meimei first.

When we all came up the room was just the same as we left, no bed was added. Then we inquired the lady and she said she was going to let us have two rooms for the night, so after we took a bath, Anor and I went to the other room which is more secluded and slept. I told to myself, "it is all so misterious like a detective novel, anything may happen." The morning we woke up and found nothing had happened. Thank God!

Menton

By Anor

MENTON is a not interesting city. We came to live there because we found the right house. But as to the city it was nothing at all. Every day we went out, the only places to go were to the beach where people sit there to kill their sickness, or to the market to see the strange things which once is enough. Otherwise, no place to go at all. The mountians were all climbed by us in one week. The theatres were no good. Once we heard that an English play was in a certain theatre. So we all got excited and went to see it, just like a country woman going to town. Well, when we got there we saw lots and lots of old men and women coming in, but none young ones. But it was quite all right. To our great disappointment the play was no good.

Everyday when we went out we could only see the old wickled faces. But no young persons were there. Mother got so nervous and moody. Every after-noon she got sad and quiet. Although the sun was bright and it was out all day long. But no use at all. We had nothing exciting, nothing changing. But we went to Monte Carlo. By bus it took about half an hour. Father thought of taking us to the movies. A big house with movie advertisements outside was naturely taken to be a theatre. So father asked the man if it was an English movie. "It is a gambleing place", the door man replied very honestly. When father heard this he ran as far as he could. The flowers in front of the house were so beautiful. Everything seemed so expensive. An orange costed Mother 2 francs. Well, it was a nice place to walk about when we lived in Menton. But comparing it to Paris, it is nothing at all.

One day Father heard that some of the Chinese friends were in Paris and so he went to see them. When he got back and told mother how Paris was and how could we go there. So we paid three months rent for one month and after two days we were living in Paris.

The Death of the Little Crab

By Adet

As THE sea waves came in, the green water changed into white bubbles and floated up the sand shore. The sea was always coming and going like that, sometimes she would carry along a breanch of sea weeds and sometimes little clams and oysters. These clams often remained on the seashore; the children might pick them up; sometimes the strong sun would burn them to death; any way they seldom had a happy ending. Perhaps one in a hundred chances the waves bought them back to the home land.

That day the sun was so warm and the water was so cool. Not only did the people like to go out, the little crab too.

Alas! it was carried away by the strong waves. Every swing took him farer away from his stone cave. His little body and legs struggled in vain. He knew not how to turn back, finally it reached the shore.

He thought of the adventures of his uncles and aunties and great grandfather with this sand shore and now he was here too! The more he thought the more he was frigtened. He was hypnotized, but the roars of the sea woke him up. He quickly ran to the sea, but it was too late, too late already, the (devilish to him) voices of children could be heard. He stole a glance and he could see the colors of the children's dresses. Suddenly the noise stopped and before he noticed he was in the hand of a child. His stomach was girdled by the fingers; he tried his scissors, but found them useless—they were too short. Now he was swang and dropped down in the middle of the air, and then something white came and caged him. He knew what it was. Oh, the roars of the waves could be only heard as whispers. When shall I return to the lovely pebble cave and talk to my dear clam brother and shrimp sister under the dancing sea weeds?

His head felt heavy and dizzy inside this stuffy white cage and from the shaking his eyes could see very little. Bubbles came out of his little mouth continuously. In the darkness he could faintly see the shadows of his village, suddenly it was all gone, but this whiteness in front of him. The shaking and swinging became higher, at last he fainted out.

When he woke up, he felt that he was no more in the white awful thing, was it possible that it was home? Under his feet were pebbles, he tried to walk out but he was met with glass. No, this is no home. The water was so tasteless. He sighed and sat still in the glass. Then he used all his strength to struggle out of this place, with its invisible cage. His eight little legs were sour and tired and so were his scissors. Slowly he went to sleep.

As he woke up for the second time, all were black. The voices of the children could not be heard. He thought maybe this was my mere chance of escape. The four pairs of legs kicked and kicked, so how he was out of the glass. How light he felt at this moment, but where? where should I go? It was all black around. Where was home? Why the roars could no longer be heard? Never mind, I will find it myself. After many falls and steep walking he could see a beam of light. He ran happily toward it though he was already quite tired down and hungry. The strong light could be seen but also the laughter of man could be heard. It didn't mean that he was near the sea. He turned around. His head was down. One step after another he walked aimlessly but still hope to find his home. Bubbles came out from his mouth again. Ah, he could see a light not as strong as the other. His feet had but little strength. And the climbing up of the high window sill made him more dizzy than ever. He was on the window sill but again he was prevented by this invisible thing—Glass! His kicking on the glass was weakening. How could he success? All strength was used up. There he lay down quietly. The sound of the waves striking against rocks could be slightly heard. But the little crab could no longer hear it for his last breath was gone.

"Poor little crab! When did he climb up here. Oh! it is dead. Poor thing." Its body was thrown into the wastepaper basket, but perhaps the spirit had gone to the waving weeds.

From South of France to Paris

By Anor

It was an early morning. Mother was the first one to get up and we followed. We all had our breakfast and soon I found our maid crying. It was the day we were leaving for Paris. We sat in the Menton garden for the last time. Father found out a new kind of flower that was blooming, everything was fine. It was eight o'clock. Louise, the maid carried the bagages for us and we walked to the station. The train came, Louise fellowed us to the train and gave Mother a bush of flowers which we had no use. She wandered hither and yon feeling hurt. Another two more minutes we will leave, so she went down the train taking out a handkerchief to wave to us, in fact to dry the tears.

Louise is an old maid, nobody living with her and therefore she couldn't help from crying.

The train started we felt rather warm and we took off our coats and made ourselfs comfortible. Mother at first loked at the sceenary, father sat and smoke, Zodet, Meimei and I read. I had a red eye and father bought a bottle of eye wash for me which I liked to drop once in a minute. When we got a bit hungry it was only eleven, but nobody could help from standing up to reach the roasted chicken. Another quarter of an hour was the promise, but it didn't seem to have any use. When it was really another quarter we have had already eaten it half through. All enjoyed more than ever. We had a nap in the train.

Nobody seemed to be anxious about what's going on, and all were so so sleepy. When we woke up it was four. Oranges, apples poured in our mouths. We got a bit tiresome. In Lyon we got out to have a breath of fresh air, and after that we had dinner. But why we had another sleep before we got to Paris. At eleven, it was raining. Father laid us to a nice hotel we did not see much that night, but heard so much of "Madeleine" from father, he repeated the word for at least twenty times that night that mother got mad of Madeleine.

The French Curiosity

By Anor

SINCE I came to France I saw many curios things which I don't see in America.

The French hide thier post boxs always *somewhere* in the wall of a store.

The French make great big, long sticks of bread and drop it on the street and pick them up again.

The French old men walk with a stick and a short cigarette and walk very slowly on the streets.

The French women count centimes one by one in order not to be cheated.

The French dine on sidewalks and on July 14 dance in the streets.

The slowness of the French beat the Chinese.

The French working couples go riding on a bycicle on Sundays and enjoy themselves.

I see French old maids two by two walking gossiping together about how old she is and what do they eat and this and that.

Ten women on the street seven wear black at Sept.

I see old women sitting on a wheel chair and pushed by any young man on the street.

I see statues of naked women and horses every where.

I see cars parking in the middle of the street.

I see old dirty houses every where in the street.

I see an old woman picking up bread crumbs and packing them carefully in a paper, and put the paper in to paper bag and the paper bag in a bigger paper bag and the bigger paper bag in the biggest paper bag.

I see soldiers walking slowly with hands in the pockets.

I see toothless women with whiskers selling newspaper.

I see all the French children wearing gloves.

I see mothers spanking children in the street.

I see on Mondays the shops all closed as if all were dead.

I see restaurants close on Sundays for the 48 hours working system.

I see all kinds of people wearing their own costume walking on the streets at ease without be looked from head to foot as in America—Turkish, Indian, etc.

We tip the ushers in the movies and tips the man

at restaurants who opens your door in the car and if you don't tip them they'd say, "Et moi?"

At stations the trains are either early or late.

I see perfume marked "Night in China" instead of "Night in Paris."

I see "pedicure chinois" every where.

I see couples kissing every where in the streets, parks and cafes.

I see brides of Jesus walking in the streets wearing the brides' dresses.

I see naked women on the stage.

I see painted faces of young girls every where.

I see beautiful shoes in the windows that I don't see in America.

The Most Beautiful Street in the World

By Adet

PARIS often boasts about her Champs Elysees as the most beautiful evenue in a world. She is not entirely lying in saying that C. E. has got the atmosphere of Grandeur and magnificence.

The essential things that makes it so grand are the Arc of Triumphe which stands straight from the one end of this avenue and who always remains grand, and the place de la concorde with its Egyptian pole pointing directly through the middle of the Arc. These two things make C. E. grand like a bridge suspended.

I can say the wideness of C. E. is the widest in the world though I haven't seen the whole world. But really these things does not matter as the important things are the cafes and the people.

The most expensive cafes in Paris are there and they are on quite a big scale with feminine musicians as orchestra. Generally cafes are divided into two parts —out doors and indoors. On sunny Sundays these cafes are all crowded with people. They sit and spend the afternon there. If you order only a *glass* of coffee you can sit as long as you please. You may be talking over things with your intimates or just leisurely reading the episodes in the newspapers. Lifting up the head one sees a continuous parade of different races and types. The newest hairdress and the latest fashions are right there promenading in front of you. I have seen a ready 2 or three time a lily-like lady walking with an wrinkled old man. A new dress cannot be kept at home but it is to be shown off on C.E. as on every blocks there are at least two cafes filled up with critictors of the passing-bys. There are also always some country people who have come to see Paris. They dressed also in their best clothes, but they are of a different type. Siamese and Arabs in their own costume come walking along. The girls are a bit timid to be looked at. There are Chinese passing by once in

a while, but English is so often heard on the road, be it either Americans or Englishmen.

We are not so Frenchy yet. As after sitting half an hour in an outdor cafe we rise automatically and leave. Then we become the one to be looked at now. Once I saw some gay men and women coming in a twenty years old car, very high and with two gigantic front lamps. They drive on the side walk for parking private cars. Many people fellowed and many others stood up from their seat to see this amusing sight. It was full of fun.

The indoor cafes has a different atmosphere. Some sat right in the frontier of the out and insides to get the two atmospheres. One of our favorite cafes is

Hungaria. A group of about 15 feminine musicians dressed in delightful colors well powdered or painted, are playing on the high stand. The tunes they play are generally the Hungaria dances and things of that kind. We always enjoyed it; for a change some gypsies would come up and do some singing and jumping, but I preferred the others.

On July 13th late afternoon we stood up on an open top taxi while passing through C. E. We saw cars in front at back and on both sides of us. The sunset was behind the Arc and made the Arc and some figures under the arc look black. Sliding down a little bit the concorde the Tullery and the Louvre were clearly seen. It was grand and worth a praising.

Once father asked us four about the spelling of C. E. without looking at the signs. The spelling is so different from the pronounciation. Neither of us got it. I got nearly right except forgetting the s at the end of Élysées which wasn't bad. I didn't forget which way the accents go.

I have always liked C. E. but I would call it too much a luxury and too much of the comfort of this world. It makes one forget all other things in the world except that is in front of you. It is extravagence of this material world, too delightful for the reality.

We Went to Montmartre

By Anor

It was a nice and sunny day. We had to go out, for if we don't we would miss the first spring day in Paris.

So we decided to go to that Church. Meimei asked where we were going. Father told her. But she did not think it was fun. So she made an artificial smile to father. So that Father wouldn't feel badly. We took a taxi, it took us about fifteen minutes to get there. I, as the usual way, got my head-ache. When we got out of the taxi I felt so dizy. Later we went to "Heaven" it was called. But it wasn't open. Then we walked and walked. After a long while we got there. Father said he became religious when he came to Europe, but the fact is that the churches are more interesting here.

As we went in Mother whispered to Father, "Y.T., take off your hat and don't smoke." We went and walked around the side and found many fascinating things. One was that was there was a picture, said to be a Jesus's face. It looked so old. Another one was not strange but beautiful. So many candles we lighted in front of a Saint. The Church was dark, the candles were bright, it made a perfect picture.

"Now, it is the world we are living again. That was a mediaevel world," said father as we came out. Peanuts were sold at every stop of the steps. If we declined the first peddler the second one would ask. So we bought one franc to safe the men from asking. They were so nice that we couldn't help from buying two francs. Father said on the way down, "We climb up so hard, so we must lost half a pound. But if we go down it is just the opposit, therefore we gain half a pound." That was nensense, we knew it. But no one could say how it was wrong. Therefore Father had a dispute with us four females. We try all sorts of reasons to proof that it was wrong. But Father answered back just as well. After the arguement Father told us the fact. And all were satisfied.

Our Concierge in 8 Rue Georges-Ville

By Adet

She is a funny person undoubtly. She looks at people straight with her brown eyes. We moved in here and there she was in her everyday light blue smock, so untidy., the old brown belt hangs loose on her waist and her shoes are loose house shoes. She, we may say, is our first acquaintance of Frenchmen in Paris.

We paid her 250 Francs each month for the smile of her face. It was higher than usual. We went down and there was this smile from her large-jawed face. "Ella, bébé, bonjour." She was kind and friendly to us in spite of her hoarse voice. We can imagine her in a street fighting or arguement. From the inner courtyard we could hear her disturbing voice. She might be washing and scrabing the brick floor in the courtyard or simply just chatting with her colleagues. But anyway we heard her voice on the second floor.

Everyday we saw her in the smock. Never a different one either outside in the Road or in the office using the electric cleaner on the red carpet. We smiled at her and she smiled at us, all very kindly. Sometimes there weren't enough stamps on the letters and she paid them first for us. When we returned she would open the office door and welcomed us in mentioning how many sous we owed her. If we had change we gave it to her, if not later in quarter of an hour she would come up and asked for it. If we give her a few sous more she gladly accepted it without haste.

Her husband was sick for the first few weeks and one day he suddenly appeared in the office, but still unable to walk. He is quite of a typical Frenchman, rather jolly and humourous. He smiled also. He is more cultural-looking than his wife. He always sat near the telephone connecter reading Ce Soir or Paris Soir. The two went well together.

Well, then, after our announcement of giving up this apartment, oh the real face was shown. No more 250 Francs a month and of course no smile for us. The woman put up her real face, looked straight at you without a smile. The man still smiled, as we passed by, very care-free. That's that and we were going to leave.

Visit to a Belgian Abbey

By Adet

OUR vacation to Belgium was about 5 days excluding the first day and the last day on train. There was one day where we spent in Brussels and the rest in the country. One day Mr. A. took us by his car to visit a famous Chinese monk in a Belgian monastery. It was about half an hour drive from the house. Amidst a beautiful forest with a public road cutting through, we were told that we had arrived at Abbaye de St. Andre Lophem-lez-Bruges. We got down and found a brand new building of red bricks and if there wasn't the tower on the church and the monks passing by we wouldn't know that it was a monastery. Mr. A. went in and came out with a monk. A nice and jolly person he was, looking very dignified in his black gown. He told us that there was just a service on and asked if we would like to see it. We agreed and entered the church gate. It is a beautiful church and very new. The gate is on the left side of the church and not at the end. There is a space before the seat and that little round space had an onion shape roof supported by several pillars. Then there was the church. It was divided into half: one half is for the outsiders and the other half with seats facing each other for the monks. It was very light and colorful when sunshine passed through the window and it wasn't gloomy like other old churches. We sat on the third bench and the monk whose duty is to receive guests sat with us and explained things to father. Soon the monks came in two by two. They were all in black and looking rather serious; they went to their seats after kneeling before the shrine. When all were seated they put on their hoods or caps which were attached to the robes. Among the outsiders there were monks also but dressed in different fashions. Those who wore brown gown with a belt in their waist were Franciscans. They had on their head but one ring of hair about one inch long and the rest was all cut. On their feet there was no socks and they wore only sandles.*

There were another kind of monks among the seats and they were Dominicans who really do work for the religion. They were missionaries in Africa and had just come back to have a vacation. They were wearing white gown and a big black hat on them, because Africa is too hot for black gowns.

It was a queer service to me. But the guest monk whispered to father and explained to father all about the ceremonies. They were supposed to have their caps on except when there was in the prayers a sentence which was expressed by God and they immediately took off their caps to show their respect to God and right

* *They had long dresses for tennis. I think they will fall down.—Meimei*

after the sentence was recited the caps were put on again and I saw in that prayer they read at that time has quite a lot of sayings from God. The sudden kneeling down of some monks meant that he had made a mistake in reading the prayers and had kneeled down to confess and ask for excuse before God. There were embracing from one monk to another like the first one A in the line embraces B and then B embraces C and C embraces D—etc. That showed the love of brotherhood from a monk to another.

It was about 10:30 A.M. in the morning and they finished the prayers at about 11 A.M. That wasn't so long. Then each kneeled down once more before the shrine before retiring. As they passed by I saw on their head two thin lines, seemed as if burned, not to have hair grow on them. Father asked and the monk said they were burned really and it is a symbol of slave to God as before the Greeks had their slaves marked. They don't burn the lines before three years of entree to the monastery and within the three years the monk can return to be a man if he can not endure the life in the monasteries. After the three years and he had decided to be a monk for life there was a ceremony of prostrating flatly on the ground to show his complete obedience to God.

This guest monk told us on our way out that no monk is allowed to talk except some very necessary things during the day. (He himself is an exception, of course.) But a half an hour after lunch was for relaxing and talking; they may go to the forest and walk and chat.

Usually when a monk wants to talk to another of something important he says, "tsi" meaning "Hey" and the other put his finger over his mouth meaning "Is it me you want to speak to?" The conversation must be as brief and as short as possible. Passing through to the hall we did see some one saying "tsi" and the other putting his finger over his mouth.

It was very interesting and then he led us to a very nice reception room and told us to wait while he would go and ask Father Loo to come.

Father Loo came in and we all stood up. He was a small but rather healthy person. He was smiling all the time and he was happy to see some Chinese children and have a chance to speak Chinese. He is over sixty already, but he looks much younger. His full name is Loo Tsen-hsiang and he was the Premier in the Second year of Chinese Republic—1912 and he was once, I think, the Ambassador to Switzerland. He told my parents all about his life and his entree to the monastery. His wife was a Belgian and after her untimely death he discovered that he was alone, no son, no wife and no parent and by the influence of his wife before her death he has come to be a monk in this Belgian monastery. His health and happiness has improved and increased since he came to this church. He studied Latin all from the beginning with this guest monk who is his manager of visiting. Father Loo was extremely humble about himself and he still speaks Mandarin with a Shanghai accent. It is a rather rare thing for a premier to become a monk. Father asked if he communicated with the Chinese friends and if he would return some day. He smilingly said he writes to his friends and he might one day return to China and lived in Szechuen where there is a monastery detached from this one. The conversation lasted an hour and we spent the last half hour with the guest monk and Ma, walking through the grounds of the monastery and visiting the school rooms. On the tennis courts there were Dominican monks (missionaries) playing tennis. Every court was occupied. They ran around picking balls in their long wide white gowns and their large-brim black felt hat remained on their heads. They shouted the scores and seemed quite content. But it was a funny sight indeed. Father Loo and the guest monk said the more they do their prayers the more they enjoyed them. But we have not yet comprehended the joy.

The church bell rang and they went to lunch. Father and Mr. A went to the general dining room where two hundred monks were seated. Mother and we went into a small dining room where we should dine. A monk came in and brought us wine and potage. The next dish was roast beef with beans and boiled potatoes. For dessert it was chocolate pudding. Mother exclaimed that how lucky these monks are from the Chinese monks. They have wine and roast beef! The guest monk told us that one day a week they have a vegetable lunch and dinners. Mother said, "That's all right, very nice." But then he said the vegetable lunch consists of either fish or duck or chicken, because of it was said to eat only of animals in the water, fish is in the water and isn't duck on the water also, and since one can eat duck why not chicken? Mother answered "Oh! I see."

After lunch we stayed in another large sitting room to drink coffee. Father said during lunch there was no talking at all and the clatterings of the spoons and forks seemed unusually loud. There was a man reading a book every meal and father thought one can hear quite a few books during the meals in the monastery.

In the reception room the grown-ups had coffee. Father Loo gave us three tiny golden piece of memory to the Church. He had blessed them before giving them to us. At about 2 P.M. we left the monastery with thanks to our entertainer and with a new knowledge of a strange kind. Though we cannot enjoy their kind of life, but were glad to hear that they themselves do. The monks said that they look at the monastery as a home, and the brother monks as a family, otherwise, life would be too monotonous. It was an impressive trip to the Abbey.

Father Bought a Radio at a "French" Shop

By Anor

"NOT ready yet," is a very common phrase to the French. But sometimes it is over said.

A month ago Father, Meimei and I happened to step into a "French" radio shop. Father said we could buy a radio, so he told the woman in the store to deliver a French one to our home and let us try and see. At 7:00 it was supposed to come. Luckly at 8:00 the radio came with much rush and "it was in time" said the man waiting to get a tip from father with a hand sticking out for money. We try and try. But nobody came to fatch it or even to come and say how do you like it. So Father went to the shop and said that he wanted a American radio and a case made to order and gave him 1000 francs. The case was supposed to come on about the date of May 20. Father phoned and phoned to the shop to tell them that they were late for many days. At last they said, "Wednesday, no doubt, sure." Wednesday slipped by and a Chinese began to wear out of patience. Father, as if he was selling things to them, marched to the shop and said, "Will you plea-s-e come?" "Yes, this evening, at 7:30. Don't worry, we will have the case ready and two American sets for you to choose!" It sounded well. But no one could ever trust the French. "Why don't you cut off the whole business?" Mother said. But the trouble was the 1000 francs were in their hands.

"To-morrow the things will be ready, prices, fix and everything will be OK." 'everything will be OK.' it was a euphonious sentence!

"Ring——" at twelve the bell rung to our supprise for it was so punctual, only 20 hours late. In stepped a man, but what do we find? Only another radio for us to try while the French one is still at our home.

"Bon!" the Frenchman shouted while he was taking his hat ready to go and self-satisfied for what he had done. "But what is the price? Where is my case I ordered?" "The case will be ready in two more days. And you listen to the U.S. radio first and I will tell you the price in two days!"

Well, he disappeared. But what was the use of trying if we didn't know the price. How can we decide?

The day will be to-morrow. But nobody believes in his coming. (No radio came after that.)

"The French make good lovers and dress designers, but no business men!" Father exclaimed.

We also bought a piano and the man was quite punctual, but when they came in they had an awful smell!
—Meimei

July 7, 1938

By Anor

THIS is supposed to be the Festival of the Cowherd and Spinster. The famous story about two lovers that meet once a year over the bridge and if at the night of the seventh of July if you sit quietly you can hear them talking. I remember three years ago Wang ma used to sit and tell us stories. In this very day she would tell us the story of the Cowherd and Spinster.

But there is still a more important thing about today. It is one year now since we fought Japan! How quick days fly. I remember last year at this time we were in New York, wondering how the war would come, and now we are in Paris, and the Chinese are about to win by the flood, I hope. Isn't it cute? Two things happen in one day.

I really was talking about the cowboy and the weaving maiden.

It was said that there was a cowboy that worked very hard and married a weaving maiden. The gods saw that both were handsome and nice hard working people. So up the couple went to the sky.

They thought that they were the nicest in the world. So the maiden didn't weave any more and the cowboy let his cows alone. The Gods saw what happened and sent them down to the earth again and every year at July seventh they meet over a bridge, the rest of the days they have to work very hard and live alone. (the birds make the bridge by grouping themselfs over the river, they make themselfs do that because they pity the cowboy and the maid) That day—today—they meet and cry and talk for a little while that the gods allow. Wang ma loves to tell these stories because she believes in them.

Morning of July 14th (French National Day)

By Anor

THAT MORNING we got up in the most unusual lateness. Because we went to bed late the night before. We got ready for the parade in the morning, and thus we went out. There was already a crowd. It was lucky that we still could get some chairs, but one cost 10 francs. We got four of them. We all stood up on the four chairs as it was impossible to see if you sat down. There were six of us, but we got on quite all right. Then we saw far beyond us groups of men on horsebacks, on foot, and music bands. Beside us lay many tanks. They were all painted mud and grass colors in order not to let the enemy see them. There were generals riding through the Etoile. There were soldiers beside the tanks. They wore blue cloths and iron helmits. They looked so ready to fight you that they looked as if any moment they might slap you. Then on top there were air-planes. It was just like thunder when they flew over. The pigeons got so scared that they flew round and round. Then there were big artillaries and all sorts of guns.

I looked over all these things and thought, "What are they for?" "To kill people." They show us how to kill people! Then I thought of the war in China, and the horrible soldiers beside the tanks. I imagined the bombs dropping down from the air-planes and all the things in action. They train soldiers to be killed. All the things in the parade were heroic but terrible when you think of what they are really for! They give that "kill people parade" to show us how the war is. That's our world!

The Bird Market

By Anor

YESTERDAY we went to the little island in Paris to look for birds. We had the idea of buying them as we entered the market but had no idea what sort to buy or how many to buy.

We walked along slowly watching every singing bird and it happened that the man called to us and told us the price of the pair of red headed birds. Father said that in these places you can bargain. They were lovely small birds all locked in a cage and we asked for the price of six birds and it was 50 francs. People noticed the Chinese and how they talked French and how they bought birds. Most people stopped and looked at Meimei. Father said it was not a bad idea to bring some home of the pairs that were in the small cage. But after a second thought we decided to walk a bit before buying it to avoid regret.

So we went out and again walked slowly. Father is fond of colors and whenever there are colors he'd take interest in them.

Now that there were a pair of beautiful colored birds. All colors different from the beginning to end, beautifully matched. Father was gazing at it all the time and at last he asked the price. But it was expensive. 150 francs for each.

Father can spend more on these for he always considered the pleasure you get out of it and the price to compare with it and if it's worth while he'd buy it. But after the thinking Father thought that if it's the two for two hundred francs he'd buy it. But the man was not interested on selling it and it made a lot of difference. So father had to let it go and we bought a cage and came back again to where three pairs were sold for fifty francs. They were beautiful and neat. But comparing to the other two they were really nothing. So finally we decided to take four of those birds by pairs and gave them thirty five francs.

Father was not contented then for he had not the colored ones although these we have are colored too but not much. Father also wished for a singing bird. One who can sing and imitate all the birds. And father was right. We all desired a singing bird.

So across the shop we went to another shop or market as you call it. There stood a bird singing so sweetly and costed 150 francs. Father asked for the last price and it was a hundred. Father said eighty for although he didn't mention it I knew that he was longing for those two on the other side.

Then between a narrow space was another singing bird and it cost only 40 francs and Adet watched that one very carefully and wished it to sing for she knew how to save money and wished that father would give up the 100 francs and pay attention to the cheap one. After a moment's struggling with the other man, father turned his head and looked at the cheap one. It didn't sing for, as father said, he was excited and it sings only when it was enjoying itself.

And father's head cooled a little about the 100 fr. one and at last bought the cheap one for after a few minutes he was sure to sing since they called it a singing bird.

After that we went again to the beautiful pair but they were sold.

So we came home with 5 birds and when I was holding it the bird sang and it made a circul of people listen to it and I felt that I was in the middle of the crowd so I handed it to Adet and walked away to pa.

We came home and put the cage on the piano and the bird sang and sang till night came and the pairs went together to each of their own branch. They hold together tightly and thus went to sleep.

But the singing bird, the one we valued most, was all alone, because he was too expensive so we didn't by a wife for him. So poor little bird, he jumped from one branch to another and slept alone. But later I saw one small bird beneath his neck and it was like father and son. Then I felt that the five were one family.

Today one red bird flew away and his wife or her husband was left alone and he or she, let us say it, it cried for it to come back and the singing bird helped it to call it back but it was no use, away it flew to the sky and no one knew where it was. But I'd hope that it was a male that flew out for then we'd have two males and two females.

I went and looked for the bird. Ah, yes, she is the lovely bird and he flew away. I am sorry for he flew away but glad that it was "he" that flew away and not "she."

The Death of a Little Bird

By Anor

My Father is not a Murderer or anything of that sort—He is an author.

The Death of the little singing bird was a very sad story and teachers would be interested in it.

You see, Father was the earliest one to get up that morning on Nov. 11th. He went to see the good singing bird and his new wife. The groom was beating his wife with his beek and what a pair!

So, Father, trying to give a lesson to the groom; opened the cage door and arrested the broom, I mean the groom. and beat the mouth of the bird ten times or so. But when Father finished the lecture to his greatest surprise, the bird was dead! So Father being scientific, tried the artificial breathing by exersing the wings. But . . . . . . No Use!

So when we learned the bad news we were all very sad.

But Father is only an author, trying to straighten things out . . . . the bird was dead . . . . Father was sad . . . . and so were the rest of the family. If anyone didn't know father he would think that father is a bad man. But no, Father didn't meant to do it, father was sorry too. I know how it feels when I do something I didn't mean to do. It feels awful, and yet it isn't your fault. e.g., spilling a cup of milk, burning in sucession four or six pieces of toast, dropping a beautiful drop of ink in front of a new dress, etc. Such things get on people's nerves and in fact these things are not to be blamed.

Father didn't get scolded but he got something even

more miserable, that is to see the expressions on our faces. Father usually says that don't explain when you argue but this time he felt that he had to explain so he did for many times he said he must have held the bird's neck too tight and the bird was such a gentle small one, and father's fingers were so powerful.

The funaral possession was Meimei and Mother. Mother almost cried. And the poor bird was thrown into the garbage can.

Radio City and Ifle Tower

By Anor

LONG long time ago we already heard of the tall buildings in America. And here we were going up to the eightieth floor. It was a warm night. Mr. and Mrs. T—— took us by the subway up to the 50th St. we got up and into the building we went. Mr. T. bought the tickets and we went into a rapid elivater. It was so fast that it would hurt your ears if you don't let your mouth open. We changed at the 59th floor and in we went to another crowded elivater. In a minute we were up on top. We steped out and walked outside. When we looked down the people were like ants and the cars were smaller than the toy cars. The streets were all lighted. It was like some boxes put together. The light seemed so small and I looked down feeling I was a giant, a god that looked down the earth from heaven, a baby who was comparing with ants. Had I grown bigger? or had the world changed? We looked at the big red light that shined and turned. Was it the sun? The sun that shined to the world. Maybe, possible. In a short while Mother woke me up and said that we were going down.

"Going down?" I said. So we went down and when we got down and I looked up and thought "Am I the ant now, or the god?" It seemed that the people up there were ants now and we people on earth were gods.

Well we went up the Ifle Tower the other day. It was triangle shape. There was no fast elivater but some sort of bus that carried you up. It was more ad-

venturious. Every inch we went upper, I felt more afraid. At last after three changes we got to the top. It was windy and crowded. This time I was feeling like sailing on a boat. The building seemed to rock. We looked down and our hands were cold and legs were sore as if we clambered all the way up. Father took us to the upper part which was the highest. There was a flag of France flying. We bought a little Ifle Tower which was less than an inch. I put my hand on top of it and said, "I am here." And Meimei had it pinned on her coat.

In Collège Féminin de Bouffe mont

By Adet

AFTER the visit to this collège, we somehow decided that we are going also. On Wednesday afternoon our parents brought us here; we were a little sorry about leaving our parents for a month, but as we saw the lovely place we began to like it. Meimei was a little bit uneasy. We brought her to the care of her teacher and then we went rowing and walking before and after dinner with Pearl and Rose and another girl. In the room it was terribly hot at night; we didn't cover ourselves at all. We didn't think much about home yet, but were wondering what they were doing at the same time. The next morning the sunlight woke us up and then the bell was rang. Anor was worrying about getting up too late, but she was much too early. We saw Meimei and she hasn't gotten quite acquainted yet. We asked a question and she always answered "good." "yes." She must be alonely there in the other maison. Frenchmen are quite funny from the Americans. The Americans are too enthusiastic and the Frenchmen too carefree. They took very little notice of us. From 9 to 11 we had our French lesson with Pearl, Rose and a few person. Anor and Pearl went swimming in the pool and Rose and I went rowing in the lake. It was very hot. Meimei was happier there with Anor in the pool. Meimei went playing in the water all the morning and afternoon. The teacher didn't take great attention in the new pupil. Meimei couldn't speak French and couldn't play with the other children. In the afternoon Anor and I went on an excursion. On the bus it was quite cool. The trip wasn't so exciting or enjoyable. We visited a porcelain musuem. There are some very gorgeous Chinese vases and bowls. Later we were laid to a Japs garden. We didn't want to go, but we went there. Later again we stepped on to a boat which sailed from St. clouds to Notre Dame. Pearl and Rose, Anor and I neither of us brought any money. The group "a little something" twice and we four sat down with thirst. It was pretty tough. About nearly eight we arrived. On the way I was thinking about Meimei. Sometimes she had the face of going to cry, but it was nice that she didn't burst into it. After the dinner with ice cream for dessert we visited Meimei. She was in bed already, looking quite sad. I didn't feel so fine either and had a feeling of loneing for home. I guess it was because of the first few days.

It was horrible at night. As we lay down there were the thunder, the lightening, and the pour of rain. The sound was enormous. Meimei must be frightened I thought. In the middle of the night there was again another storm, but I went to sleep anyhow.

Today I woke up and hoped it was cooler, but it was almost the same. We had our French lesson. It was quite easy. Then came a letter from our parents telling us about all the things. Meimei came up and she read the letter. She said she wanted to write to them and she did. She looked more happier today, and she talked besides just answering. She said she like to be in the same room with us. It was very natural, because even we liked to be at home. The lunch was quite delicious. Our parents didn't phone us as they said and Meimei was disappointed. The girls here are of different nationalities. Some are quite nice, but they don't come to talk to you often (and I don't blame them at all).

(August 10, continue)

On Sunday afternoon mother and Father came to see us with Mr. Chu. We waited impatiently for 3 o'clock to come. When one's dearest people are separated, one never thinks of their little faults or mistakes but always of their best points and imagines them as a perfect personality. It is funny and that's the way I felt too. We sat in the room and talked about all things on both sides. A-ching's (our maid) romance with A-cheong is getting quite serious. Mother talked lots and lots about her getting marry. Father brought us three little carry-lead pencils for us and mother brought us oranges and cookies. We enjoyed every minuit of their presents. Later we strolled a bit in the garden and they went back. We weren't sorry truely, because we have arranged to come out on Friday afternoon!!! Well, that's that.

Ah-ying and Ah-hua were said to be here day before yesterday, yesterday and today, but they didn't appear. *Maybe* today they will come. Day before Yesterday night at table the teacher talked to me about China and all and she didn't know that China is a republic until I talked her.

Yesterday night was fine and well-spent. It had rained in the whole morning and just cleared up in the late afternoon, as you can imagine the air in the evening. I went walking with a girl named Tania. She is fifteen also. With some people one has to think out something to talk about but with some like Tania the conversation just goes on without any special effect. We talked about different things. She is frank and easy to deal with, rather nice.

Ah Ying came late day before yesterday night. She had a coiffie and it looks very nice. I played tennis with her yesterday afternoon and she is just learning also. So we did a lot of picking up balls and that's all.

I liked the teacher better gradually. She is nice. This afternoon they are going to see more tapestry makers. We are not going because going out with a group there are always a lot of waiting and hurrying.

(Aout 31, 1938)

Yesterday it was Mother's birthday and we weren't able to celebrate it. Today I went on a promenade with a Mlle. and some kids. At first I was told that we were going to Domont which is about 9 kilometre back and forth. I was a bit scared, because it would be quite tiring. The teacher then said we may turn back as we wish. Today it is quite good for walking. There is neither the sun nor the wind. On the way there were a lot of beautiful apples and pears. Because the mlle. was present we weren't able to enjoy eating roadside fruits. The road was fine and easy for walking. There were some gypsies on the road, very dirty with their hair untidy. They asked us to let them read the lines in the hand. An old gypsy woman was sitting on the grass looking strangely up. Her face showed her age years of long travelling and moving in the little cart.

Not before long we turned back and arrived at school at 3:30 which was just nice. Irene—a white Russian girl brought me to her room directly after the walk and told me to write something in her album. I couldn't think of a thing after a long walk, so I brought it up to my room and promised to write later. I just wrote something on it and it was: (Both in Chinese and English)

"My country is in Far East and yours in Northern Europe and we meet here in Bouffemont. Isn't it wonderful?"

I dread writing on an autograph album because I never know what to write and especially in an unfamiliar schoolmates' since maybe we were together just for a short time. I won't be able to write "hope our friendship will remain forever or don't forget our short happy days together," because we are bound to forget or separate. It is nice of course to have the autographs of old time friends, but it is rather odd to read only of friend's writing in praising and admiring oneself, of which many may not be as true and as sincere as they sound. Well, but I write false ones too.

(September 3—38)

On the 1st (Thursday morning) I was called to telephone at 7:30 A.M. Father telephoned and told us to come back on the same day, because he was too lonely since mother went to Brides-les-Bains. Meimei, Anor and I were glad to go back that day instead of the next day. We were all pecked up in less than an hour.

We have come home and it is so nice though we miss mother more then in school. But she will be back in a week.

London

By Anor

LONDON is the place where I wore the first pair of long stockings. You see, I didn't bring enough socks over so the only thing was to borrow one of Adet's lysle stockings. It needed garters. So I used father's garters and anyway they can't see them.

It was a funny feeling, I felt like a half grown-up person. It was like a long something in a long sort of something. Anyway I enjoyed wearing them. It was like Christmas stockings with my legs in them.

Well, I do think that I am crazy by talking about my stockings rather than London.

But anyway I am going to begin talking now.

We are very extraordinary people. We decided to go to London in ten minutes. It was very quick and we had fun packing for it was unexpected.

So that very night we started for London. We went by the boat train. Do you know that the three of us threw up everything we ate and father was in another compartment? So poor mother had to get up and get things for us. We all didn't get a good sleep. And think what mother asked Adet in the midnight. "Adet, did you pull the plug out when you finished ironing?" It worried mother very much and mother always thinks of these things.

After 9:00 A.M. in the next morning we got to London. We were all land-sick except father and Meimei. Then we went to a swell hotel for a friend recommanded it to us. Then we all took a bath and jumped into bed. We slept till 2:00 P.M. in the afternoon to get over that night's torture.

Then we walked a bit and went to the wax works museum.

It was so mavelous. They had Hitler, Roosevelt and Mussolini and King George's the sixth and all the great men and women. But some of them didn't look like them at all. They put the Duke and Duchess of Winsor seperated from the royal family. They made Mrs. Simpson very fat and ugly and short.

The next day early we went to call on the Ambassador as a rule. We had supper with them.

After the call we got to the St. James' Palace to watch the changing of the guards.

They were like tin soldiers and had those great hats on, and had red coats. They had music bands too.

Then we went to Westminster Abbey. I hated the stone coffins which you had to pass and under the floor where all the coffins were.

But anyway I went in to say, "Yes," when people ask, "Have you been to the Westminster Abbey?"

In the afternoon it rained. We went to the London Bridge to sing, "London Bridge is falling down" but we did not sing it.

Then we went to see the crown jewel, you know, the dimand that is on George VI's crown. But unfortunately it was closed. Mother and we were all disappointed.

But then we went to tea. We didn't think it was the regular English tea for we didn't eat much.

Then we went to take the "underground" or subway in America. We enjoyed it for we have to take the escalater to get down. Don't you think we are very Chinese to enjoy that?

Anyway I say I like English subways better than American or French. The American ones have to make such a rattle and the French have an unbearable smell.

The third day which was Sunday, we went to the Scott's for dinner. It had very good food. Then we went to the newsreel. It was very good and very very good for me. I liked it too much that the next day I kept on saying to Adet, "The newsreel was very good, wasn't it?" She had to say "yes" every time or I would keep asking that. Anyway I asked on just the same.

Yesterday—the fourth day—the last day, we went to see the crown jewel again. This time we got in. It was almost as big as half of an egg.

In the after-noon we went to the ZOO! We saw many animals. But you've seen them before, you know, the tiger has four legs and so has the lion. The fish swims in the water and the lions don't and all that. You don't need me to talk about these. But anyway I tell you that we went to the zoo.

That night when we came back the sea was very smooth. We didn't know a thing and this morning we are home again. "East or west, home is best."

Hitler

By Anor

I HAVE not learned how to make a diplomat speech. I dont expect to go to Germany. So I dare and can say plainly just what Hitler is. He is a liar, a poker player and a mad man. The world would probably be at peace if Hitler's mother didn't give birth to Hitler. Hitler had once lied about a war and made father stop working for five days. That five days' working might earn $100. That $100 might be given to the Chinese war. With that money they might go and buy bullets and guns. With the bullets and guns they might kill 100 Japs. In those 100 Japs one of them might be a person like Hitler. With that certain "Hitler-like" man in Japan the world might have another great war with two Hitlers in it. That might cost death to 1,000,000 people.

So, at last, Hitler might cost death to a million people. Just think how many persons were stopped working during that war scare? Take the minimem—1000 people. Let's multiply 1000 great wars by 1,000,000 people to die in each. That makes one billion

people to die in the future great wars, if my arithmetic is right. So Mr. Adolf Hitler might kill 1,000,000,000 human beings—NOT COUNTING THE HITLERS TO BE BORN BY THE HITLERS. That's 1/16 of the people in the world!

Hitler Played Us a Trick

By Adet

It was really quite something during that war-scared period. Everybody in Paris, London and many other cities was bluffed by this Herr Hitler; Of course we were five among them too. Oh, everything seemed so sad in those days. I guess there must have been artists mourning over the last days of the glorious Paris. Looking back now we seemed such fools, busying over luggages and hurrying for passports, visé, but circumstances forced us to be so and it wasn't our fault. It was Hitler that made us pack and unpack for nothing!

It was funny though that the sky seemed to indicate the coming misfortune. It was raining all day on that Tuesday, the 27th when news was changing every minute and when it got to evening the rain stopped and the sun came up casting a strange scarlet light over the whole city. If there was a Chinese fortune-teller in Paris, he would get some meaning from it about the crisis.

Every one was reading or buying the newspapers everywhere. They seemed anxious to know the news and at the same time afraid to learn it. The Frenchmen were shaking their heads and shrugging their shoulders this time and on their faces they lost there usual carefreeness. Even on Avenue Champs Élysèés usually frequented by the parades and tourists looked so piteous. I guess the tourists must be worrying over the tickets to get to homeland. The colorful neon lights didn't help to cheer up the minds; they looked like the last glances of a beautiful thing that was dying out. Sad, sad it was!

Father was really serious about getting away. Mother

thought maybe there wouldn't be any, but father had convinced her that it would be better to get away soon if there was going to be one. So the family was mobilized. Father went out to the steamship bureaus trying to get some information during the mornings and afternoons while mother was going to the bank and getting a few things before we sailed. We, the three, were dragging out suitcases from the closets and discussing about the arrival in New York. For two days we passed like this. We bought 50 kilos of rice and several bottles of cooking oil and packages of salt—the essential food in case food should stop coming into the city and also bought candles in case light was put out; really at the time we were packing for the first boat we could get to America.

The two things were rather contradicting, but we did them. At last we got some thing about the boat: there was the Ascania sailing on the 5th of October; two spared rooms just right for us, if it shouldn't be confiscated for transporting soldiers. That was something at least. We would be going to Le Havre that week-end to wait for the boat there. So we started packing. Father packed his books with us and we packed the clothing with mother. All the apartment was full of boxes, papers and trunks and at night we slept in the room with nothing on the table, empty drawers and suitcases. Meimei was so excited with the idea of going to America again. I asked her whether she would prefer to have no war and stay in Paris or have the war and go to America and she replied, "I'd rather have war." We all said she was too selfish and told her about what war means. She said, "Yes, I know, but I like to go to America." I was both glad of going to New York again and quite sorry for leaving Paris.

Well, one more thing we had to get though was the visa of the American consulate. The passport room was jammed with people. Everyone tried to go through between the other people and if you stood on the table you would see lots of wriggling heads all getting nowhere. Father went there and waited for a long time before he was told to have six photographs of the family. Father hurried home and we ran to a near-by photographer. The next morning early father went again to the American consulate to wait his turn. He telephoned back saying that he would have his turn about eleven. Mother was in the Chinese consulate already trying to get some kind of seal for the passport. I was to get the photographs and rush to the consulate. I got the photos and arrived at the Consulate just about eleven. It was about two numbers before father's; we sat and waited for mother's arrival. Two minutes later mother arrived with the passport. That was nice. Then father and mother went in and I went home.

Days before we had already seen trucks distributing fine sand in front of every house. That was for putting out fire of incendiary bombs. The proclamation to call back the reserve soldiers was pasted on the lamp posts of the streets. The husband of a servant in the building had gone already and we heard the babies crying early in the morning before he left. War was really coming.

We sat in the parlor and turned on the radio on the night Hitler was speaking. We were so anxious. First there were the roars of cheers to excite the people and the listeners. We were indeed excited. While Hitler was shouting at his highest voice, father listened and translated it for us. It was about half past ten already when the speech was finished. The impression of the speech was very bad. Father shut up the radio and exclaimed, "There is no God in this world! If there is one he would certainly make Hitler's heart stop beating in the midst of his speech for the peace of the world."

The slight hope for peace was all gone and we were really leaving for America.

Suddenly came the conference of Munich. "There is hope in it, there is hope in it," father said. True it was. "PEACE" was on the first page of every newspaper followed by some photos of the big four signing the pact. We turned back to look at all the luggages we had packed during these few days. We all sighed for the waste of our labor and at the fact that we had to unpack all again! But realizing unpacking was better than a war, we opened our trunks willingly. Now we had wasted time and money on account of this Hitler. Anor and Meimei were rather disappointed at not going to America. Everything went back to routine and joyous faces appeared again.

There was one thing that was good about the crazy days; that is, to get a little taste of the great war in China and from this little experience to know the feelings of real war-time people and refugees at home. While all the time busying over our own things, I had been imagining the real war, the real killing, the real fear in China.

I shall end up by a little joke some friends and ourselves talked about. Father said he was going to send a list of personal expenses including sous and centimes to Herr Hitler. A friend said he would certainly turn it to old Dr. Benes and blame the fault on him.

I Got 6 Brothers and Sisters

By Anor

THE day before, our family was changed to eleven instead of five. Why? Can Mother give so many at a time?

Well, we went to Mr. Loo's office. There were fifty photos of children waiting for us to pick. Those children were war orphans waiting to be supported. 720 francs for a year to serve a Chinese child which is around $20 gold, 5 cents and a little a day!

We were anxious to help. So we at first looked around the pictures to see which ones were good. Mother insisted that the five Must be Boys for Mother has Not got any Boys. But father said that girls were the same and it does not matter to him if they were boys or Girls.

But every time father said, "Ah, there's a good face," every time it was a girl.

At last we chose about eight and then compared them. But none of them really looked like us. So we had to choose strange faces. Some eyes too small, forehead too small, face too big, too rough, etc. But we had now chosen some good ones. But they were all boys. Father said that was no good to choose all boys. So some one picked the girls out and father chose one. She was cute and somewhat shy. There was another one whom Father said was a better girl. But we couldn't choose between the two so at last we took six.

So we came out very satisfied. We took out the pictures and looked and looked and looked.

One is the shy girl, one is the better girl, one is a strong loud boy, the other is a small boy of ten, the other a big-eared boy, another with triangle eyes and that is all.

Father said after we got home,

"What is the use of money if we don't help but always keep it to ourselves? One must be useful and helpful."

Mother continued,

"One must not think that I am important. Always I, Me, My, you must consider others too."

Then after a while father looked at the pictures and said,

"After all, can they really be our own sons and daughters? No. Just put the three big boys together and just see how they'd fight! Girls are better after all."

Mother said,

"No. I will not have them to be our OWN children, the three girls we have is enough, only I do wish to have a boy of my own, not those orphans. Suppose those boys turn out to be rotten eggs."

"But it'd be nice one day to have them all together with us!"

"That big one can eat three bowls!"

"And imagine how he'd laugh."

"And I don't believe every one of them can study well."

After all those conversation, we decided that we would not have them to be our own. But helping is a good thing to do.

Part IV. CHINA

Our Garden in Shanghai

By Anor

TODAY as I am sitting here, the breezes from the window blew in and made me thought of our beautiful garden in Shanghai.

It was spring. The roses grow on the wall of our house, everything in the garden was blooming. The grapes were growing, the tomatos in our garden were getting bigger everyday. The big tall trees were green and handsome.

In the morning before breakfast we used to have time to walk in the garden for a few minutes. Mother would go and examine all sort of flowers and see how the peaches were growing. And sometimes go and pick up some tomatos for the kitchen. Father would walk slowly with a hand holding Meimei and tell her to listen to the birds calling. Adet and I went busily picking up roses and many other flowers. The fragrance of the flowers went right into your nose. Everything was beautiful. The pigeons were laying their eggs on top of the house. "Look, a new rose is coming out of this bush!" Mother would say. In the afternoon about two, all the servants went to the garden, sitting and chattering about their friends. Sometimes we could hear laughter and whistling among them. We knew they were enjoying spring among themselfs. The maids were more kind to us. The cook would take a longer time in going to market. The gardener would stay longer in the garden. It was Spring! We stayed in the garden without knowing the time. Now we left the beautiful garden to an apartment. The garden now, I suppose, is ruined. But lukily in Menton we got a garden something like it. With orange trees which we girls clambered everyday for oranges. Flowers for us to move the plants from one place to the other. Everybody was caught by spring again. In the afternoon the family took two chairs out for my parents to sit. But how about us? Each finds herself one seat on a tree! A seat on a tree! Father brought his notes out and imagine the characters in the novel under a tree. Mother took out "Gone with the Wind" and was hidden with it under the same tree. We three sat on a tree. Adet and I tried to memerize a poem. But how could we with all the spring surroundings! Father excused us because it was spring!

Our Garden in Shanghai

By Adet

Our house in Shanghai had a very nice garden around its three sides. On Edinburg Road there was a long narrow lane which led to several residences—including one of ours. We took that house chiefly because of the garden.

There were the vegetable garden on one side and the lawn on the other, while in front of the house was a courtyard with two basins of Lotus flowers.

I shall describe the garden as the seasons changed. Spring was most popular in our garden. Everything came up to receive it. The peach trees bloomed and all the little flowers struggled out between the bricks. It was most fun. Mother would be very busy in the garden planning where to plant the young flowers. The sun was fine and usually after lunch on Saturdays and Sundays we came out to the garden and saw about the plants. The sun made all of us feel warm and sleepy. And we had to take off our sweaters.

We have three peach trees in our garden. They bloomed gorgeously. But about getting peaches they were not worth anything. In each tree there would be 5 or 6 tiny sour peaches. We were told not to touch them till they grew sweet and red. But nevertheless we picked about two peaches each week trying their taste. Each time it was sour and we had to throw it away. Then, you see, by the end of spring they were all gone. Though we never got any peaches, we enjoyed seeing it grow, bloom and fall. Soon the peaches would be on the market and we would forget all about our own peaches. On a peach tree there is always some sort of jelly on it. We often picked the glue and played it in our hands. It got less sticky gradually. Father likes this kind of material very much and he often played with it in his hands also. Later the thing got quite dirty and mother would say, "Oh, throw it away." We then threw them away without pity.

Surrounding our garden all around were the tall poplar trees. They grew so fast each year. When spring came they began to grow little green buds from their bald branches sticking up in the sky. The leaves grew bigger and bigger and the outside view would be entirely separated, for usually in winter we could look out the window and see if our car was driving in or not. In the later part of march we had to start the cutting of high branches in order to get more breeze in the summer and not to be entirely fenced up. There are about 40 trees all together, and it took about 3 or 4 days to do all their coiffure. Ah-ging and Ah-gung would be very busy, in fact the whole house would be busy. Ah-ging and Ah-gung would be on the trees sawing down the unwanted branches. Tai-sou-fou (the cook) and his wife would sit on a stone and chop the branches into several parts for burning for the whole year. Mother would be so busy instructing the two A.G. which one to saw and where to put them and all that. We children, coming home after school, looked around and took odds and ends for ourselves. We would try to put up something in the garden. Father wouldn't have much part in it. He would just come out from his study for a little rest and look around and discuss with mother.

There were two trees that were especially tall. They were too tall for reaching and each year we saw them grew higher and higher and just sighed. They grew over the wires and still kept on growing and they will reach the sky one day, as Meimei said. The trees didn't seem to mind being over height. They looked down upon the cut trees and laughed. When there was a storm or big wind, these trees swang east and west and their leaves made such noise. They certainly made us feel the seasons more.

As I said before, we picked little odds and ends. We took these sticks and tried to fence up and cut up a piece of ground. Our names all contain a "Ju" in Chinese and now we wanted to make a garden of our own and would call it the "Three Ju Garden" which is San-Ju-Yuan in Chinese. The first thing was usually to fence it up with sticks. We had to use tools to make holes and it also had to take quite some work to dig a hole deep enough to make a stick stand. We took all sorts of things and worked very hard for a whole afternoon. The fence stood up at last, with the help of stones and ropes and threads. But there mustn't be a storm or a big wind, because otherwise the whole fence would collapse. That's what father means by a children's work, but we were satisfied. The next morning if it

was a Sunday we would work on it again. We transplanted little plants of flowers into "our garden", moved stones into the garden as stools and all that. Then we must decide where to write the name of the garden. We generally used a cardboard and wrote big San Ju Yuan on it. It was fun. Then we invited our parents to see our work. That was the most glorious time of the garden. Sometimes later we continued to add decorations to it, but they gradually dropped off. It all depended on us whether the garden lives or not after a storm. If we rearranged the fence, that meaned it was going to live.

In the same old place near the swing each spring we made the garden, for until winter season it was again just about a piece of ground, sometimes with the cardboard dangling in the air. That is the little history of our San Ju Yuan. It has faded away since we left Shanghai.

About the flowering season of our garden, it was most gorgeous. All the little flowers which we thought had died off last year budded up again. First bloomed the purple ivy flowers which were just outside of father's study. They bloomed quietly.

When the leaves against the wall were multiplying, we knew that the roses were coming out. Oh, the roses of our garden! They were in so many types, small ones, big ones, some last long, some last a little while. Anyway it gave our garden a glorious time of three weeks. Mother worked in the garden in the mornings, if she had time in killing and taking off the little green worms on the rose branches. They must perish or else the rose buds would be eaten up before they bloomed.

Then they bloomed gradually. Mother never allowed us to pick the early flowers. She liked them on their natural branches. Until there were too much on the walls of the grape vines, we picked them and put them in vases in the parlor and all the rooms. Sometimes when our friends or relatives came and mother would scissor some branches for them. In these weeks a rose was almost nothing in the garden. All our maids picked them and fixed them in their hair. Gorgeous it had been really. We showed it to our friends, proudly, and how they admired! *

* *There were some wild flowers sticking out. They were very pretty. I sometimes picked them for Mamma. And sometimes liked them to stay there.—Meimei*

But about the end of the 3rd week they began to drop and fall. They turned yellow sometimes. The ground under the rose vines was just full of flower petals. It looked empty on the branches without the attracting red. In some spots there were one or two late roses, look more beautiful all done. When they were gone too, there would be only the thick leaves and summer would enter.

The willow trees seem to fit so well with the summer. On them there were the cicadas singing all day long. Sometimes when there was some wind and the willow branches waved as if going to bend and the cicadas waved with them. They looked so harmonious. The cicados sang all day long without fatigue and sometimes since they had been singing so long I didn't hear it. I sympathize with the butterflies and cicadas in all the fables. Just because one was jealous of their lives one began to create stories of them. Aren't butterflies working while we think they are dancing and aren't cicadas laboring while we think they are singing? There isn't anything for the bees or ants to be proud of. One imagines a poor crutched butterfly or a thin cicada begging food in the wind before the satisfied bees or ants, but actually the butterflies or cicadas never live to winter. And they have their own lives and why should they ask the bees for food?

Well, well, well, we picked the empty shells of cicadas clinging to a little branch of willow. We liked them so and kept them in a drawer in the corridor. They were so clean and well-shaped. One day maybe in November, we reopened the drawers and saw the dry shell and some half eaten by the cockroaches and it reminded us of our joy in the summer picking and keeping them.

In front of our house there were two jars of Lotus which father bought from City God Temple. They were about two and a half feet high and two feet in diameter. Every summer the lotus bloomed in the most beautiful fashions. They were big and pink and later when they dropped we got lotus seeds to eat. In some early mornings before breakfast we walked a little bit in the garden. The air was still of a very early morning. The grass was wet and the plate-like leaves of the lotus had many little water pearls on them. We bended the leaves and the pearls rolled down. Little pearls grouped into a big pearl and big pearls divided into many small pearls, and then the sun shined on them. The lotus flowers were fresh as if washed by some cooling spring water. "They have come out of mud without being spotted or dirtied." Lotus seeds were delicious; we pulled layers before we got to the meat. It is a food that takes time to eat it.

In the jar or basin, about ⅔ was of mud and ⅓ of water. Under the heavy cover of leaves there was once a combat. Behind our house there was a little dead stream and after the spring shower it swelled up. And the 3 inches fish began to multiply. They were called "fish of five hairs of whiskers" because on their mouth there were 5 hairs. It was so easy to catch them because there were so many of them. Once we caught about 4 or 5 of them with the help of nets and cans. We put them in the lotus jars where there were already some baby frogs (tadpoles). The fish cut into the mud and disappeared. The baby frogs were a bit disturbed at first. But we thought they were all right. After a few days when we looked into the jars neither the frogs nor the fish were there. We were very surprised, but we saw little holes in the watery mud. Sometimes the fish came up again but never were the frogs. They were eaten or beaten by the fish. Now the whole jar was their world and they were the sovereigns. They slipped in and out freely. But when autumn arrived they disappeared with the flowers also. Soon there was no lotus nor lotus seeds. The two jars were them removed to the garage for the winter until spring.

The summer storms were liked by us a lot, although it sometimes blew down one or two branches and sometimes ruined our "San Ju Yuan". As it is, it was always intolerably hot before a storm. Every one in our house would be shouting at the heat. The flowers in the garden needed watering everyday. At 4 or 5 o'clock in the afternoon Ah-Ging would have to take the water hose and connected it up with the faucet. In those hottest days we would relieve his job willingly because we were then in shorts and allowed to get wet with the spray. Father joined us often. We both watered the flowers and man to utmost satisfaction. We saw the drying flowers wake up again and our sleepy nerves also. Mother sometimes came to the garden and watched us, but she never joined us because she is a grown-up. We were allowed only half an hour of this playing, but we would be all wet already and squeaking and shouting. Meimei avoided and at the same time liked the water. So there were running-aways and catching-ups and all. Then later in the bath room taking our baths, we heard Mother, Wang-ma and Cheou-ma shouting, "hurry up! and close the window. The laundry is out-side! hurry up!!" We were excited in the bath tubs by seeing through the window the dark heavy clouds. In a minute the rain was here. In the yard we watched the raindrops: one big drop, two drops—soon the yard was all wet. We sat or lay in the covered verandah watching the rain and the coming storm while drinking the cooling bowl of sweet green peas soup. The wind increased and the rain also. Then there came the lightening and thunder. The bamboo shades flied up and down and the surrounding trees shake also. Inside dark and cool, we were seated in the parlor wondering if the Chu Yuea (a kind of flowers like Peony) could stand it. All the servants in their little dining hall were fanning and appreciating this storm. But when the thunder was a bit too loud, Cheou-ma would utter, "Ah-ya!" The supper would not be uncomfortable and sometimes we wouldn't even need the electric fan. The storm would die out but the rain continued all night. In bed we heard the rain and the numerous cryings of the frogs in the neighboring field.

The next morning we woke up; the sun was out already. The Chu Yuea was still all right though a little bit bended and the new branches had been bended and broken quite a few. The sun was hot and the flies and mosquitoes returned.

In our vegetable garden we had planted different vegetables in turns. The tomatoes, cabbages, beans, corn and cucumbers. The cucumbers were most successful, I think. They were on a vine of some old rotting woods. They grew each year and we got a pretty lot of them. The tomatoes and the cabbages weren't as sucessful as the cucumbers. And yet we took so much care. They lacked some kind of furtelizer. The tomatoes grew so slowly. Mother often turned up the leaves and examined the thumb-size tomatoes. Later on I don't remember eating them at all.

We planted the corns in about April of the year we went to Lushan. They shooted up so quickly. We couldn't imagine that little piece of sandy ground could really grow things. Father wants us to see the fun of nature as he has had in his childhood. It is really interesting to see things grow. Then when they were just about going to grow corns we left for Lushan and in Lushan we had post cards from Ah-ging reporting the life of the corns and we were so sorry to hear that the servants would have to eat them or else they would be rotten to wait till we came back. We weren't able to eat them. When we arrived at home after the vaca-

The Over Grown corns

tion we could hardly recognize our little vegetable garden. The corns had grown over a man's height and so tight and closed together. There were still some hardened corns which were no good to eat. Well, then afterwards mother told Ah-gung to cut them down for another planting.

When cicadas stopped singing and lotus seeds were eaten, then suddenly came a cool wind which announced the arrival of autumn. Fans were left in the corners and everyone came out to receive the west wind. All the spring and summer flowers were practically gone. There were but heavy leaves all over and some sour grapes on the vine which were half eaten up by the sparrows. The leaves on the tall trees began to fall and the ground was all cover with them. The sun was always bright and we spent much of our time outdoors on Sundays. We sometimes even prepared our lessons outside which were usually not as well-done as indoors. Wang-ma was pushing Meimei on the swing, while Ah-gung was sweeping the fallen leaves. The light wind was blowing Meimei's hair. "Put that sweater on, Meimei, this wind isn't just nothing!" said Wang-ma.

"Ya, truly, these days I have to sweep the leaves every other day regularly. They are falling fast," uttered Ah-gung while sweeping the leaves to a corner.

"Yes, in a twinkle of an eye they'll be all gone and winter will be here." replied Wang-ma. Soon lunch was announced and we went in. On the table we found big, fat crabs lying in a plate. There were vinegar and ginger on the little plates, and there we began to eat this famous specialty of the season. After lunch we would all come out to the lawns including one or two friends or relatives who had stayed for lunch for we always had guests on Sunday lunches, and have tea there. We sat on rattan chairs which were moved out from the garage and the elders talked while we played on the miniature sliding board or croquet.

As we followed our guests out, we met the flower planters.

"Come, come, Anor, go and call the planters." mother said.

The flower planters were hurrying along. Mother to father: "Don't you think our garden is getting colorless now. Let's get some chrysanthemums."

"Fine, it's just the season for it, I like good ones," father replied.

Mother was busily directing where to plant the 32 plants of real chrysanthemums for 2 dollars. They were extremely cheap for all the joy we would get out of them, as father considered. In an hour all the 32 plants were then planted. The planters went home with their empty basket and the two dollars happily, and we were going into the house satisfied with the new plants.

The chrysanthemums bloomed soon, and one or two of the gorgeous yellow ones would be transplanted to pots to be placed in the parlor for glamour.

After the chrysanthemums the garden was empty. The trees though not in a twinkle of an eye, were already bald. The swing, though didn't get balder or leafless, looked so pitiful in its surroundings. Meimei seldom went to swing and we too. Sometimes from the window I saw it swing a few times back and forth with the wind and disturbing the threads of the spider-web.

Soon the white frost came and followed the north wind. It was the lonest time in our garden. Our breath could be seen in the cold air and we all went red-nosed.

"ho-oo-o-o" was the sound we expressed in our garden before entering the automobile.

But when winter really was there, it was different. The only holly tree began to grow red buttons and the young bamboos and the only tree of plum flowers monopolized the whole garden. The plum flowers blood-red reflecting on the white snow, was father's choice. When snow was falling we would be all in the garden—capped, coated, muffled and gloved. Trying to make a snow man or throw snow balls was rather difficult, all wrapped up.

We were often disappointed on the snow which wouldn't stick or last and we weren't able to play with it. I remember once when we had just come back from school, it began to snow quite heavily. The sky was extremely black. Just about 5:30 P.M. Father suggested that we might go to the Jessfield Park and see the snow. The car was driven out of the garage and we five started out to the park. At the gate there were only two doorkeepers. They were waiting for the time to close the park. We inquired about the exact time of the closing of the gate in order not to be lock up in the park. It was quiet in the park and there were nobody but two other persons who knew the joy of the time. Mother and father and the three kids threw snowballs to each other. Mother enjoyed very much also. We printed our shoesizes on the smooth untouched snow. We wandered quite a distance till the time was up. Our coats were wet by the snowballs and when we got into the car my fingers were numbed and to be numbed was quite fun also. I got a feeling as if the fingers didn't belong to me. That time we got the full enjoyment of snow and we returned to our garden and we saw there was little snow which hardly covered all the ground. It was a sad time in our garden, I suppose.

Later we sat around the fireplace warming our hands and eating baked chestnuts forgetting all about the garden. That's that. But soon the spring will be here.

Why I Like Chinese New Year Better Than Western New Year

By Anor

THE Chinese New Years have many things which Western New Years don't have.

In China, New Year is count as the biggest festival of the year. All the people, rich or poor have to dress up and go out to the streets and see the circus or fair.

Now that the government had stopped the fire-crackers we lost a great part of the fun in New Year. But in spite everyone still does it.

I will tell the whole story of how we celebrate the New Years both Chinese and Western.

According to the usual western calendar, New Year is a week from Christmas. So we always have a tree in the dinning room. Of course we have hundreds of New Year cards to stand up on the mantle piece. And when the wind blew it was often my business to stand them up again. Then we went out to a movie or something and come back for a better dinner. But often parents were invited to some one's home. So that was how we past an uninteresting New Year and nothing could make the western New Year more joyful.

As to the Chinese New Year, if you don't want to celebrate it, you can't help from enjoying yourself.

Three days before the maids would wash all the

clothes and the cook would roast pork and the boy would clean the floor. Why they do this three days before is that they say that if you do those things on New Year day it would wash away all the good lucks for the coming year. Then of course the streets are all dressed up. Resturants are not suppose to close so that on the New Year day all stoves are being repared so they could have the excuse and go out for some fun. But really they are all right.

The City God Temple is the crowdest place. Everybody go there and buy things because it is the cheapest place of all. You can buy anything from birds to noodles there. Beggars come and you have to give them food or money because on that day everyone is suppose to do good things.

Early in the morning we get up and have the prettiest dresses on. Servants come with their good clothes and bow to us for three times which looks very funny. We wrap two dollors each with red paper to give them, or one dollor and one cent, we are suppose to have every thing evens.

Instead of coffee we have a kind of very delicious tea (Dragon eyes). We have red eggs which our nurse love to dye them. She uses red paper to color them. They look just like Easter eggs. Each one is to have two. We wonder around the whole morning while each of the servants take turns to go out. On the afternoon father usually takes uss to City God Temple. It is really not a temple but a big gallery. There is a restuarent which has only vegetables. And they make artificail chickens and ducks out of the vegetables. The most fun is in the evening.

We have big red candles on the mantle piece where

Grandmother's picture is. And we have rotating lanterns which we bought in the afternoon. It is a candle in the middle. Around it are a circle of silhouette cars and persons. In front of the persons or stage players we have a paper and on it we have a stage. The candle burns and has warm air which makes the 4 persons around turn and the shadows of them shine on the stage so that we have persons going around the stage.

We have a splendid meal which the cook is willing to make for it is *Chinese* New Year. After that we sit around the fireplace and talk. It was said that the later you stay up the night the longer life your parents have. Soon we stay up until eleven or twelve. But I think the whole business is really nonesense, in spite we do it just the same for we wouldn't be so nice going to bed at the usual time. Then we take out the mahjong for the servants to play. Because we don't know how to play it. Well it happened that we have five servants and the game is for four and luckily for them that only four know how to play and the one who doesn't is Chou ma. She is so good that she alone goes up and do some work while the rest play. They each take out one dallor and thus the game started.

We talk about this and that while chewing mellon seeds and eating water chestnuts. At ten the fire crackers sound. We buy the most loud ones. We have many kinds. One that is called "Sky Earth Crakers". We put it one the ground it sounds on the earth when we light it and then jump up to the sky and sounds another one, and I don't know where it drops. Another are small ones, we tie them together and they burn from bottom to the top and sounds. There are so many other kinds, some that are not cracker but have flowers out when you burn them.

Father and mother make special effort to stay at home with us that night.

Now, what do you think is better? Chinese or Western New Year? So one would be silly if he doesn't celebrate the Chinese New Year. More over, we have paper dragons that are about two blocks long and lighted with candles and goes all over the places. We have endless things to show. So nice are they that you can forget the whole world. Three cheers for the Chinese New Year!

Chinese Movies and Movie Stars

By Anor

CHINESE movies are not as popular in China as U.S. movies in America. But just the same there are Movie-Queens and Beauty Queens among the stars.

We rarely go to see the Chinese movies, only the very good ones. The trouble with Chinese movies are that they don't have good theatres. Many people think that to go to a Chinese movie is a low class thing. But it really is a pitty Chinese actors and actresses are just as good as any other countries. I know the reason why the ordinary people don't go to see Chinese movies often. They think that everything must be foreign. So many go to see Hollywood movies, and since the ordinary people don't go to see Chinese movies the lower class do and the ones who don't know English go. So the theatres are not so clean as the other movie theatres. It is not that every English speaking person doesn't go to the Chinese theatre. Of course there are some who go, but less. The reason why less of them go is because they don't get talking about it when you say that you have seen a Chinese movie called so and so.

But don't think that everyone who go to a Hollywood movie understands English, they go and laugh when people laugh and even louder. Just to let the ones who sit beside her or him think that they know English.

It really is terrible when a real Chinese asks you have you seen such and such a Chinese movie? Also I think that the servants at home think that we don't want Chinese movies. I say why I am more for Hollywood movies is that I go to see them more, not that I don't like Chinese movies. There use to be soundless Chinese movie, then it is different, you have to read and at the same time look at the motion pictures.

As to movie stars there aren't as many as in America, but also countless. The most popular one is 'Butterfly', she looks a little like Loretta Young, then there is the "Beautifulest Lady of the East", Chei Lie, she is not like any American stars. Then we have the girl who played in a film I heard that the film came to U.S. Her name is Cheng Pigeon. She acts very well. There are a great many more of them but I can't name them all. These three I think are the most popular ones. And there is another, Wang Ren Me. People like her but I don't.

Men stars are just ordinary handsome men that I hate.

In China it is not hard at all to see the stars. I once

met "Butterfly" as they call her everywhere, crossing a street in front of a d^partment store. She has often been invited by any common people without any camera man and after all you think back she is the most well known star in all China.

Wong-ma

By Anor

WONG-MA was the nurse of Meimei since Meimei was born 10 months. She was a rich familie's girl. But became poorer and poorer later on. I will tell you the whole story.

Wong-ma was born in Nanking. At seventeen she married a diplomat. She was proud of her beauty and said, "When I was a bride people looked at me and said, 'the bride is good looking, not too tall or too short, but her feet are too big'." Then she said she got up in the middle of the night and tied her feet in order to get them small. But when it was the revolution, her husband died and she was only 26 years old. So she run to a Christian school and had a class, later on they made her the principle. There she got sick and they gave her opium. "It was in the evening, one night," she said, "I sat at the church door and heard people singing in the church. I listened to them and later on they were talking about the harm of opium. I got frightened and went in to tell them I smoked opium. The pastor told me to go there the next morning. So early the other day I went there, the pastor told me all about opium and told me to lie in bed for three days without any food and get over the bad habid," she continued. "That time I was staying with some of my friends and they came and called to me, "Wang Ta Chie, why don't you get up." I didn't tell them I was correcting the habid but told them I had a headache. In three days my blankets were all torn up by me and I saw a vision he said to me, "don't be afraid my child you will get well" and it venished. The next morning I got up and was all well. I told my friends about it and they said "it was Jesus." When she wanted to continue her story we felt uneasy because did she really see Jesus? I don't believe so. Maybe it was imagination. Then she stayed teaching there but people said that she was still young and found her another husband who was a fruit dealer. She went with her husband to Shanghai and stayed with a mistress. But later she didn't work with them.

One day when father was in Europe, Meimei's nurse was kicked out because she kicked Mother! So mother told one of my uncles to get another nurse for Meimei. So he went to the place where all servents out of job were. Wong ma was not staying there but was passing there and was chatting with the boss of the place. Sixth uncle said he wanted a Nankingnese, but unfortunately there were no Nankingese. The boss said to Wong ma, "Why you were borned in Nanking weren't you?" So Wong ma fellow 6th uncle home. She was fat, short and quick temper. But has patience. Meimei was so hard to take care of in those days, a cup of milk would take her two hours to drink. Wongma went with her around a big curcle and fed her a spoonful.

I was the one she hated most. When she did something I hated I would tell her and she would come back in a red face and yell to me.

If she says the chicken should be cooked now and mother says no do it in the afternoon she would immediately say of course in the afternoon. Well a thing like that would make me feel so mad so I had to tell her she said the chicken should be boiled NOW.

Anyone would look at her and said she weighs about 150 lb. but she insistes on saying she was thinner then mother. If we said she does something wrong she wouldn't listen and went to ask mother. Once she was sewing the blankets for us. I saw that it was the wrong side but she said it was right, so I went down and asked mother, luckily for me I was right. You ought to see how she hated me and scold me because she hated mother. She said, "This Second Miss! People are busy enough. You have no business to do with this sewing blankets, and you have to come and pick faults. I'll go and ask the tailor to see if this is the right side!" She yelled at me for I saw she was wrong first. Mother heard her shouting and scold her back. And I felt so happy!

Chu ma

By Anor

CHU MA is the wife of our cook. She is now about 33 years old. So timid and shy. Wong ma acted like the boss of the servants at our home. So Chu ma was afraid of her. The cook and his wife had fights over each other, the cook used a long hanging stick to beat her, she would run to another room and the cook came after her. Such things happened quite often at first, but later on mother threaten them by saying mother wanted to fire them and so they got better.

Chu ma was suppose to do the laundry and ironing. But the cook made her wash all his dishes. Poor Chu ma, she was so weak at argueing.

She earns $10 a month. According to the Chinese it is very good. The cook went to gamble almost every night. If he lost he would take some money from the food and if he wins he would buy a three penny needle for his wife and two flowers costing him two pennies for Wong and Chu ma. Once when he lost almost all his money, he took it from Chu ma's selary which made Chu ma hide all her money in mother's drawer. But the cook could see that mother ought to give his wife money such and such day so he would ask Chu ma where is the money. If she didn't say well there will be a fight. Wong ma is such a busybody, she would get angry for Chu ma while Chu ma sat and cry. It all seemed to be the cook's fault. But some times when the shy woman gets angry it would also be frightful.

The trouble with Chu ma in summer was that she had an ugly smell. Oh, anyone can't bear it. Wong ma being contented with herself scolded her to us every day thinking that mother's favorite is her. And it was because Wong ma had been working with us for very long time. And Father's favorite is Ah Tsing.

All About Ah-Tsing

By Anor

TSING means gold, and "ah" just an "ah" so that tall servant we had is called ah-gold. We will call him Ah Tsing as in Chinese.

Ah Tsing is a tall, faithful, nice servant. To start with I am going to say how tall he is, not in feet and inches but as Meimei say, "When Ahtsing stands in on that mountain there in Hangchow his head would touch the sky." It gives you an idea about how tall Ahtsing is. He is a Tongchowese. He was first a rickshaw boy. But later when mother saw that he could be a regular house boy mother made Ahtsing a house boy. There was once a very interesting story about him and a horse.

As Ah Tsing one morning got up and was wiping the chairs and tables, there was a China horse which was a valuable thing but not as valuable as As-Tsing thought. I don't know how but Ah-Tsing happened to break the legs of the horse. You ought to see how he felt, as if he had stolen a diamond and was caught by the police. So he burried the legs in a corner of the garden, thus he throught he was save. But when we got down for breakfast he kept quiet. But when mother saw what had happened and asked him he said that the wind blew it down. But mother didn't believe him and wanted him to tell the truth. So Ah-Tsing did, as he is *not* the kind of man to tell lies. Mother told him to dig out the legs and we kids helped to deliver them into the house which I suppose he didn't like. But it was all right, father had a kind of thing to mend the legs and I think he regreted after for what he had done for he got a scold from mother.

Henceforth Ah-Tsing had nothing to be complained about. There is another interesting thing about Ah Tsing and his own leg.

Ah Tsing got some sort of queer rheumatism. And according to his standard he had to cry at midnight for the pain.

He wanted to borrow 90 dollars from mother to go back to his home town to cure the pains but imagine, what was the use? Shanghai is better to cure this long spelling name, "rheumatism" than that small town of his. But Tsing didn't listen to mother and she had to let him go. After the vacations he came back and saw no improvements. Mother told him that she would pay for the doctor's fee if he would do as mother told to go to the red cross hospital.

But instead he went to a temple and asked the buddha for help. He said that the buddha told him to write something on a piece of yellow paper and paste it before his bed so that the devil wouldn't come. So he did but what was the use? At last he did as mother told and got well! He regreted what he had done again.

All these don't make him to be father's favorate servant. But there are many particuleir things that did made him a perfect servant to father. The most thing he did was that he wanted to learn English, and read novels, wrote beautiful words in Chinese. He asked for new words.

He often came to Adet and asked what did this or that word meant. He often told me to teach him English, to start with one, two, three and four. He bought himself an ink cake and a Chinese inkstand so that he could practice his charaters. All these made father so happy. He sometimes mentioned to go to a night school after all the work at day.

Father presented him a dictionary as a reward for all this. He sometimes went to the book stands and buy novels to read. But Chouma knowing nothing at all throught it was just a little something about books and didn't think that Ah-Tsing wanted to get education, so she often threatened to through Ah-Tsing's books away. For she hated the tunes Ah-Tsing sang out as a Chinese always does when he reads aloud. I think this is the most important point that father liked him best.

On the other hand he also knew how to play with us children to amuse us with all sorts of things.

Then he is a very good house boy, for instance to call telephones and answered telephones. He even learned to answer, "wait a minute" when a foreigner called and also learned from Adet to say, "Mr. Lin is not at home."

The only thing that father thought the Ah-Tsing ought to learn was when he was talking. You just can't stop him. He went so quickly one sentence after another for so long that at last when he stopped you don't know a thing he was talking. For example, one day we told him to buy a wooden trunk for books and when he came back this was the conversation.

Father: Well, have you bought it?

Tsing: You see Mister, I went to such and such place to look for it but they said it costed $3.40 and I said it was too dear so I went to many stores and they were all too dear. I ran and ran till my legs were sore and went on till very far and asked for it and then at last

I got it for $1.20 and you think mister I ran so much.

Well after all all, Ah-Tsing had to say was that he got it but with great difficulty. The speach he made above was only a short and clear one. For if you'd hear him! He was not complaining about the distance he ran, but he was just a long speaker.

I don't think all this mattered. But anyway father liked him best.

Soo-chow

By Anor

IT WAS noon, Saturday. We were tired of staying at the big city. Father proposed of going to Soochow. So we hurried and packed as fast as we could. In half an hour, we were in a car going to the station. It was two hours in the train. We got bored and played games. At two we got into the city. Stayed at Garden Hotel. It was always the hotel we went to. Then after we have cleaned up and washed we went walking toward the river. To a boat, by the way of getting to the boat we had to walk in a narrow street, probably the narrowest in the world. It was about one foot wide and a man weighing 200 lb. could not walk in that st. or path. After getting though that street we arrived at the boat house. The boat was not the kind like the Central Park rowing boat. It was red wood. In the middle of it was a room. Back was where the boat women cooked our lunch, and did the rowing. We sat at the front. The boat was so clean that we all took off our shoes and took a nap if one felt sleepy. It was always August when we went there. The crabs were so delicious. A big crab as big as half foot not counting the feet. Our boat women were so good at cooking. And no one could be more contented then that. The breezes blew on your face. The smell of cooking went in your nose. It was so peaceful. Some times we got up to see the temples and flower girls come and sell us flowers. We ate and felt like heaven. At certain times we had to be pulled by the ones on shore. The scenery was magnificent. It was much better than Shanghai. Peaceful quiet and simple. Father told us stories about his youth. But no one thought of

a little corridor we had to pass through.

the Japs. The Japs that ruined our country. The Japs that put gunboats in the river instead of boats for week ends. Machine guners instead of flower girls on the shore, bullets instead of crabs in the river. The beautiful flying birds are all to be air-planes. The Japanese don't know us, they can't find our peaceful world. Anyone can get along with the Chinese old fashion boat women, but who in the world can ever get along with the ones who tried to maintain peace in China by bullets! Well, maybe the Japs pin bullets on their coats instead of flowers!

Soochow

By Adet

SOOCHOW is the city where we often passed our weekends. Hangchow was nice too but it took a four hour train to get there which was too much. Often on Sundays early in the morning we started off and returned late in the afternoon. I shall tell one of these Sundays that we were there. But these Sundays were planned after being there as tourists for a few times. We had found out the best ways to enjoy Soochow.

One Saturday when we had returned from school for lunch and we were discussing what we would do this weekend, Father said, "Let's not go to movies this week. If the weather will be fine to-morrow—how 'bout Soochow?" He turned his eyes toward mother and us three. Our eyes were shining bright and our mouth could not keep from opening a little bit to show our delight. Mother smiled while drinking her soup. "All right, if it will be sunny day." The three now really laughed out and showed their delight. "Let's go again to the Stone's house boat." "I hope they will be free to-morrow," etc.

The afternoon we would stay at home patiently with no asking "Shall we go out this afternoon?" Adet and Anor would hurry to prepare their lessons knowing that if we do go to Soochow, we wouldn't have time for the lessons in Sunday.

The next day it was bright as can be. Anor jumped from the bed and skipped to mother's room and asked, "Are we going to Soochow today?" Mother was not entirely awaked yet, but father whispered, "Yes, we are." Soon Adet and Meimei woked up and learned the happy decision. "Wang-ma, we are going to Soochow to-day, we are going boating," said Meimei. "Oh, really, fine, you are going to put on a beautiful dress today." "No, no, not a beautiful dress, because we are going outing," I replied, as Wang-ma's imagination of our trip was quite different from it really was.

Soon we were all at breakfast table, Mother said, "Bring along only sweaters, it will be sufficient." We caught up the nine o'clock train and arrived there at eleven. A horse carriage led us directly to Kwang-tsie Choun (a bridge) where the house boat of Stone's family was just below. Through a tiny little passage we went into the inner road. Passing through this less 2 feet wide passage we always mentioned that Mr. X (fat) could never pass through, even he went sideways.

Father and Anor had ran along to the bank where their house was situated. Meimei and I was walking behind with mother, for mother's high heeled shoes weren't so comfortable on the pebble road. In the Stone family there were a mother, two sisters; the elder one with her face pocked, very sharp, the second one much nicer and gentler, and a little brother around 10 years of age.

Father said, "we have come again." The elder one replied, "fine, fine, come on the boat, come on the boat." We came along and said, "How do you do?" to the boatsmen. We have known them since the hotel introduced them to us and each time we came to Soochow we always took their boat. The whole boat itself was made of a very nice wood of crimson color. It was divided into two parts: the back is the kitchen and the place where they oared the boat forward and in front there were three places—the boat front served as a seat or a nice place to take a nap. The covered deck where we generally were and where we took our lunches and in the center of the boat there was a little parlor or dining room all cover and with glass windows on the sides, but we preferred to stay outdoors and used it only as a cloak room. Father arranged with the sisters the tour of the day, the price and the menu of the lunch on the boat and also some pastries for tea. Mother added some dishes she liked and we relaxed.

Soochow boat

The boat front was so, so clean that the sisters took off their shoes before stepping on it, afraid of making a shoe mark on it. Father went up again to buy some peanuts and Soochow candies while one of the sisters was doing her marketing. We were hungry already and father and mother assured us of a good lunch as the food of Soochow boatswomen were very famous. We the children had taken off our shoes already and walk on the slippery floor of the boat front and as soon as father returned, he took off his also.

A man was hired to help the rowing for it would be a whole afternoon trip. The Stone family were all in the back including a little kitten and the Lin's family in front. The narrow river in the Soochow town was very crowded and it turned around a lot. All the house boat for hire were parked there and the transporting boat loaded with mountains of cabbages and cages of chickens, were passing through all the time. Our boat got hit by another larger house boat and the pocked elder sister stood up and put her hands at her waist and began to curse and scold. Her whole flow of phrases came out at once and with her sharp voice, all the people in the surrounding boat turned around and looked. The woman on the other boat was not too gentle either and she had her phrases and curses. While muttering so loud, the two boat passed each other and soon we were far apart. The sisters came down but continued to say, "the devil—" Both of boats were not a bit hurt, in fact we didn't know it until we heard the shouting. The thing could be ended by just saying, "ha, be careful." It was quite a scene or a sight which people talked about about Soochow. All the feminine Soochow accents came out. We were rather amused by it and I think so were the voyagers on the other boat.

Soon we have come out of the city and mother took off her shoes also and we were so happy. We were going around the rivers around Soochow in this beautiful boat. As it got away from the city, it was quiet. It was about 11:30 A.M. We sat there in the boat front and talked of all things. At the back we heard the sound of cooking and the talking between the hired man and the sisters. On the river there wasn't much traffic. Once in a long while there was a steamer passing rapidly and left its smoke and noise behind for us. There were the houseboats passing along and we looked at them and they looked at us, each saying in his heart, "So you are on a boating trip also." But the people in the other boats were generally more formal; they sat in the parlor and had their shoes on. Maybe it was because they had guests or far relatives. Besides these, there were the real boatsmen whose only property was the boat and they transported turnips and new spinach as their means of living.

Sitting on the boat lazily we heard the sound of the water jumping under the boat. Soon the lunch was ready and the pocked sister came and asked if we would prefer to stop while having lunch. We suggested that under the big tree over the other side of the bank would be a nice place to park the boat and have lunch. We all stepped up the bank and took a little walk while the sisters were laying the table, except mother who preferred to chat with them easily on the boat. The air in the rice fields was as soothing as possible and we saw the riping corns waved to and fro according to the wind. Some country boys were playing "glass balls" on the ground (The game was to deliver a thumble-size round ball from the finger and try to hit other balls in the center). Under the shade of an aged tree, some lying on the ground some sitting, they all shouted up if it had been a good hit. We came back to the boat and saw the dishes were all out. Mother said, "Come on, or it'll get cold."

One of the famous dishes of the boats women was fried shrimp. They had learned to do it with such skill. It was fresh and crispy and not hard in the mouth. Every dish we had that day was delicious, though it wasn't a feast or a complicated and rich meal. We all had second helping of rice. After lunch we had the hot tea which washed off all the greasiness in the mouth away and the Soochow candies. These candies were special things of Soochow and they were so famous in Shanghai and the nearby towns. I cannot describe them but any way they served as wonderful sweet pastries with tea. We had to relax after the hearty meal. On the little table in the middle of the covered deck there were the tea pot and the cups with peanut shells on the saucers. We three lay flat on the boat front and as I let my hand down outside the avancing boat, I touch the water cutting another line on this peaceful water. Mother was having her after dinner cigarette and father his cigar (at that time, not pipe). We were quiet for a while. The sun was shining on us, but it was just warm and nice. Later I gave my seat to mother and Anor gave hers to father. We sat up and played games with toothpicks. On our way there were many little stone or wooden bridges. They were always ones of the "32 bridges surrounding Soochow town" which the sisters had told us. Passing through each bridges we always tried to look for the name of it imprinted on it. Some of them had faded out after enduring years of wind and rain. It was fun. The afternoon would be spent in a quiet mood, though we were enjoying every minute of it. Meimei even took a nap on the boat front. When she woked up she said, "Oh! ha, ha, I am here," and we all laughed. Then we began to talk about things. We talked about our education when I grow up and then poor, old Mr. C with no one to care of and then we critisized of the sisters on the boat.

At four o'clock the younger sister brought out two little dishes of cakes they had made. These were Soochow cakes made by its specialist. They were "powdery" as we called it in Chinese and it means smooth and agreeable like good English angel cake. We were approaching the town as we were having tea and there after tea we had to get up and leave. It had been a wonderful way of spending a weekend leisurely. The Stone's family bid us good-bye and hoped to see us soon, as they always got good tips from us.

The two hours in train passed fast and we were at home in a while. Wang-ma came smiling along and asking Meimei, "Was Soochow enjoyable?" "Yes," said Meimei.

We took a bath and had a light supper at home and while sitting in the parlor, we couldn't imagine we were in Soochow this noon on the Stone's boat.

City God's Temple

By Adet

THE CITY GOD'S TEMPLE is in the heart of the so-called "Chinese City" in Shanghai. It was most crowded in holidays and Sundays. The country people got up early in the morning and came to this City God's Temple to enjoy themselves for the day. They went back at night to the country and continued their farming early in the next morning.

In Sunday mornings we sometimes went there. Our car drove us to the gate of the busy place and we started our walking into the city. The real temple I really don't remember seeing it; I think it is just a ordinary popular temple. Surrounding the temple were all the little shops selling little cheap pens and rings, checkers and mahjongs and birds and fishes. The streets were extremely narrow and some of them were covered with oil cloths.

Entering the gate there were the little jewelry shops. Little false jade rings only cost 10 cents and yet it looked so real. Fans with perfumed wooden bones, little figures for miniature gardens, silver charms, and all were so fiscinating even to us who had lived in Shanghai for ten years. The noise was quite big along the streets. Since there are so many people, there are always a little child missing his mother who was busy arguing the price of a chains of ivory pearls. Then there in the midst of the cloud, she would discover the little one was not beside her, and some idlers would tell her that the child went that way. The child and mother would meet and the mother would slap a few times on the back and shout that why he didn't follow her. A scene like that is quite common in the temple. In a radio shop there was always a radio opened wide loud and the cracking voice swang along the whole street. There was always the atmosphere of festival in the town. The real old jade shop was very interesting also. They had their jewels all wrapped up in velvet pieces and locked up in little drawers. These shops seldom sold unless it was a high price. The shop keepers spent some time on arging the price and if the customers didn't buy, they wouldn't mind. They seemed proud to have those precious jade bracelets in their shops.

There were also the portrait painters and seal cutters. From a small window one saw a calm man sitting very still cutting the seal with heavy eyeglasses. There was a low lamp shining on the stone.

One wandered along the streets watching people and things and then he came upon a noisy corner with mixing chatterings and twittlings of all sorts of birds. Once in a while, there came a sharp voice of a parrot from the inner corner. The other birds weren't afraid at all and kept on chatting. It was the bird market. They sold big birds as big as fighting cocks and small birds as small as sparrows of a thumb size. Father bought several pairs of yellow and blue birds. We kept them in the garden, but they died off gradually. Near the bird market was the animal market where they sold dogs and cats and turtles and Java fighting fish. It was quite smelly and dirty there. Next to them was a quiet market—plants market. It not only did not make any noise, but also gave out fragrance.

In this city of God's Temple there was a lake of big fish, and above it was the famous "Nine curve bridge." It was a bridge that turned nine times. Only the idle people stood on the bridge to look at fish and feed them. The water hadn't been very clear, but people still stood on the bridge and looked at fishes. Along this lake were the famous restaurants. There was one vegetarain restaurant which was very amusing. On the menu there were roast chicken and fried pork, but actually when the thing came it was made of beans and mixture of vegetables and yet they looked so much like chicken before you tasted it. If somebody didn't know that it was a vegetarian restaurant, he would think that the liver tasted more like bean-curds than liver. Restaurants for little eating or pastries were very famous there also. Certain restaurant for wontons, certain one for sweet cakes, the goumets had figured out.

City God's Temple was such a rich and peculiar town, quite typical of rich towns in China, and yet now it is but a town of ruins and horrors.

Summer Resort in Lushan, Kuling—1934

By Adet

I WAS eleven; Anor was eight and Meimei was four when we were in Lushan that summer. We stayed there for a month and we were very sorry to leave that place in the last day. Kuling is a famous summer resort in the Lushan mountains; it is practically a town 4 or 5 thousand feet above sea. Very cool indeed it was there.

I remember quite vividly the first day we were there. We took three sedan chairs. Mother occupied one, Anor and Meimei one and I myself one and the bearers preferred to carry me because I was the lightest. But really I got up and walked several times to let father sit for a while. Sometimes we climbed together and let the sedan chair be left empty. Oh, it was very stiff climb. Often on one side of the narrow road straight down a hundred feet there was the babbling spring. It was frightful indeed. In some of the steep part, mother got up and walked for it was safer to walk then to be carried. Anor and Meimei were tied with leather belt and they held their wet hands together. As we were reaching the top the cooling breeze increased. Father with his stick said proudly, "how is my suggestion, good?" He awaited our sedan chairs' coming up and asked each person in the chair. Everyone's answer was "Good, good indeed."

The traffic was quite heavy. When two chairs were passing each other, the carriers went very slowly. It was lots of fun to be in a sedan chair. It swung a little when the carriers took a step. The carriers had a funny language. When one person told another to slow down he didn't say slow but some kind of a shout. They sang a tune all the way up; one sang and the other answered. "Huna ho," "Hah-a-ho" and so on.

The trip to the top was about two and half hours and we stopped several times at the midway tea house to eat some oranges and drink some tea and the carriers also had their tea. Then we began to see Kuling in the mid afternoon. Many lovely houses were seen. We went to Chinese travel bureau to inquire for hotel for the present. We were led to "Fairy Glen hotel." It was lovely. Guests slept in little bungalow by themselves. It was extremely cute. We took two bungalows. Anor and I took a house and Meimei slept with the parents for she was too small to sleep in a house with her sisters alone. Each little bungalow had a little verendah, a little waiting room and big bedroom and a toilette. Meimei made a famous remark on the bungalow which we don't forget. She said, "At night, you take a rattan chair in the verendah and turn on the light and read a novel. Isn't it wonderful?" She was four and couldn't read and yet she knew the joy of reading a novel in a rattan chair placed in the verendah at night.

After a little rest in the houses, we—Anor, father and I, sneeked out to the guggling spring in front of the hotel and had our first "wash of feet", while Mother and Meimei were sleeping. What we meaned by "feet washing" was to take off the shoes and socks and wade and played in the water. Father was so happy when the cooling water was running through his toes. "Ah, See, that was how I spent my childhood." We were so happy too. Then later father went in and had a look at them. They were awake. Meimei was displeased that we didn't call her. Father brought her to the spring and she was laughing blissfully.

That night we really slept in the little house by ourselves with thrill. We woke up quite early and from the little laced curtain of the window we saw the white clouds rising from the opposite valley.

On the next day we got a villa for the summer. It was a small stone house in the middle of a hill, surrounded in three sides in woods and one side facing down the hill. The next day after we moved in father discovered that there was a little dug-out in the corner of the house and a small stream of water was running down into it. Father felt that he could do something about it. So while Mother and I were unpacking the things the other three worked on it. It was originally just a hole and happened that there was a stream of water running down. Father tried to make a little pool out of it to "wash feet" when one didn't want to walk far. Father spent two days and half on it and it was made all the sides were places with stone pieces so that the water wouldn't be muddy. Father was extremely satisfied with it, but as he is a mental worker and seldom uses his musles since he left college, he got a sour hand and couldn't write for those three days because the hand was shaky when he took a pen. Mother smiled and pityed him. "Poor child, he does not have any strength." But father denied it; he said he was the (1st or 2nd or 3rd) winner of a race of half mile runner and he was in the second foot ball team of St. John's College. Anyway the little pool about 1′ by 1′10″ x 1′6″ was very useful for the whole Summer. The water was always full and very pure and yet it never overflowed. We didn't use it to wash feet for it was too little, but we used it as an ice box. We dipped oranges and apples in it and bottle of honey water also. We usually dipped thing in in the morning and by after lunch those oranges or melons were as icy as can be all through.

On one of those refreshing mornings, Meimei was going to get her bottle of ice water and she discovered a green and orange worm in the water. She was frightened and she shouted. We all came out to see. It might be called a beautiful worm or frightful worm as one pleases. It was a rare kind of worm, seldom seen even in mountains. We didn't know how and when it got there but anyway it was there. Father got it out and removed the water in the pool with a pan in fearing that it was poison by chance. The pool was empty. But two hours later it was filled again by the tiny whispering spring. And oranges and apples were put in again.

There are different queer sorts of insects in the mountain. There was a kind of insect whose body and feet just looked like twigs. It was indeed hard to see him on a tree. We caught one once and put it on a tree and saw who can find it fast. It was hard indeed.

Then we once caught a "golden Beetle". It was very beautiful and of the golden-greenish color. We tied a string around its stommy and let him fly around and around. It was cute to look at it flying but later we let it go to prevent it from dying out of sorrow.*

From the city to our house there are two routes: one short cut by streneous climbing, the other nice road but comparatively long. When we were too tired we

* *I remember that he stayed there for quite a few days. If I call it I will call it a "frightful and ugly worm."—Meimei*

took the short cut though it was very tiresome, but it was all right to have oranges waiting for you at home. The passage was rather woodly; there are wild berries and crickets in the bushes. Mother usually preferred the long way, but when going up the shortcut father often helped her up. We each had a stick including Meimei who was often carried by father. I always dropped my stick at least 2 or 3 times when we went out. When I dropped once mother would say: "Aha! once." Then I would try hard to keep it in my hand. But some what it slipped again. Anor accompanied me in dropping sticks once in a while. Once when we were "washing feet" my cane slipped down the spring and father had to hurry down to get it.

We shone our own shoes, about every other day after breakfast and we took out all the dirty white shoes and put them in the small verandah. Some carried shoes; some carried shoe cream and cloth. Since I was and am the oldest one I had to wash the white shoes and let Anor and Meimei put on the white cream. Sometimes when the dirt didn't come out by brushing I dipped the whole shoes into the water and then played with it. While we were shining shoes we talked a lot like a sewing party. Anor had the best part of shoe-shinning. All she had to do was to put cream on them. Meimei had to do the walking part. She carried pair by pair to the stone bench in the yard to get sunshine. The steps laid down to the yard was difficult to take. Meimei didn't mind walking. She took one pair down and then came up again when she would be saying, "What were you saying." We told her about it and then told her to come back soon. It was quite a delight to clean shoes at that time for we had leisure, leisure in the mountains.

In the afternoon when sun was a little westward we started our shopping or walking or wandering. Sometimes we went to town and had ice cream in the little tea room. I clearly remember that I saw a picture of Ginger Rogers on the dainty wall. I thought from my

The family "washing feet"

English studies I learned that "Ginger" was a kind of untasty plant, and foreigner used it for a name, isn't it queer? Later I found out Ginger Rogers besides being a forigner is also a star.

The town was pretty small and there was not much to see, so we often took walks along a stream and whenever we saw a nice spot where there weren't many people we went down and washed feet. We always picked a large rock to put things on. Mother when she was in a jolly mood would take off her socks and dipped her feet in the cooling water by father's persuasion. We waded in the little pool trying to find beautiful pebbles. Once Meimei slipped on a pebbles and sat down. Her pants were wet and on our way home she went without her panty. It was a strange feeling, she said, without pants.*

In the evenings, it was so peaceful. Sometimes when we came back from a long trip we felt happy to be at home in pajamas. It was always quite chilly in the late afternoons. We had the water boiled, for there wasn't running water, for bath, and we all changed into pajamas and slippers. The maid would bring the oil lamps up from the kitchen; there were usually 3 or 4 lamps lighted. We carried a lamp around to the bedrooms or parlor. It was fun indeed to see a room lighted by the little flame. The cook might not be ready for dinner yet, and we sat in the parlor talking and playing games. Some sat by mother's side and some by father's. We often followed mother around to see if the bed was laid or if the dinner was ready or if there was any biscuits left in wall cupboard. With the lamp around and our parents, we were not at least afraid of dark. The rooms were so much attached.

In Kuling our parents were never invited out at night except once. It was a real rest what they wanted and they got it. During dinners we had lots of fun. The dishes were real hot and tasty. Meimei always sat beside mother and sometimes even in her lap. She was small then but quite independent. She was very slow at eating. We always told her to hurry. But mother said, "never mind, let her eat." The lamp was on one

* *I don't remember.—Meimei*

of the corners of the table. There were little insects flying around. We saw some of them fell into the lamp and died. Some of them got dizzy and fell into the dishes, but that was rare.

After supper when the maid had cleaned the table, we sat around this useful table again. It was a desk, a dining table and a card table. We played cards, simple ones like Joker, Donkey and memory. We enjoyed them I think more than others enjoy bridge or porker. Some games Meimei played and some she didn't. Then she would say, "I shall sleep, while you play cards," and sleep in mother's bosom. Some times when we didn't want to play cards we played chess or other games. Anor was usually good at it.

We always loved to hear our parents talk about things when they were boy and girl. There would be New Year tales or school funs or the first time they met. All the personalities in the little home town would be dragged out. "Oh, what is Bread-teh doing?" "O— he is still there, just the same." "How 'bout xxx sister-in-law?" "Yes. She is in Singapore with her husband and is earning big money." Conversations went on like this with much humor. Then about going to church in lines. There were the girls in one line and boys in the other. When the big boys saw that the girls were on their way also they would tell the little boys in front to hurry. Father was the little boy then and was the leading one. He did as they told and ran. The teacher saw it and asked father and a another boy in to be scolded. It was unfair indeed, as they didn't know what was wrong about it.

The views in Looshan were marvelous. In the morning we saw the heavy clouds flying over the valley and then after the clouds were gone there was the sun again shining bristly on the green mountain side. There were colder mornings when the clouds entered our house from the opened windows and doors. It would be a little chilly and misty in the rooms and we had to close the doors and windows for a moment. Near the little town there was a pavilion for looking at sunset. Once we went there and sat in the pavilion to wait for the sun to come down. It was a tiny place with stone tables and stools. There were a group of picnicers. We said to ourselves that we must come here and picnic but some how we never went there. The sunset was really gorgeous, mixed with all kinds of red and yellow. There were somewhere purple appeared. It was a magnificent sight.

There were also the Pine Walk. A road quite high in the mountain, beautified by the pine trees on both sides of the road. The walk itself was covered with small pebbles, flat and clean. In the late afternoon a stroll would be wonderful and as the wind blew the whole group of pines waved hither and yon. They made a sound like roars of a faraway sea.

In Kooling it seldom rained, but, when it rained it poured. They came so sudden and quick. The raindrops were enormous and wetted the ground in a twinkling of an eye. The sound was pleasant to ears, unlike the May rain which we call women's rain, thin and small and last a long time. It was grand indeed like a hero on his horse galloping and it cleared up soon after about quarter of an hour. If you were outside on a trip or something when the rain came, it would be impossible to keep dry, even under the heavy-covered trees.

At home when we saw the rain was coming we hurried and put pots tubs and pails outside to receive the pure and sweet rain for cooking or washing to save the trouble of the man getting water from the well and carrying it home. The raindrops made different tunes and notes on different receivers. It filled up so quickly. After the rain our little pool always swelled up and we would pour some away to keep its level. Sometimes the rain came in time before our baths. Mother allowed us to wade or walk in the rain and let it fall on our body. It was great fun especially in that place.

During our stay in Kuling we took about three or four long trips to visit the famous places in the mountain. We usually arranged two sedan chairs and took turns in riding on them. The cook we brought from Shanghai often went with us also. Starting from home with baskets of fruits, towels and water, we went on our journey. Up the steep mountain and woody hills, there are a lot of old places where certain famous authors used to live and where the kings and princes used to pass their summers. When we arrived one place there were either the monks who took care of the place or the sedan chair carriers to tell us tales about that place. There was a old temple where a Ming prince used to keep his book and a fashionable temple were everybody visited if he was in Kuling. It was said under the stone floor of the main hall there was an old dragon. It was said true, because if you used your stick and knocked the stone floor in a curl line sounded hollow. The line was just in the shape of a dragon body. There were wild lilies and pretty flowers on the roadside. In order to pick them we had to run ahead before the sedan chair caught up with us. It was rather hot at the mid-noon walking outside so sometimes when we saw a nice stream we took off our socks and dipped them in the water. It was extremely cooling. On a trip we often took lunch in a temple. The monks served meat also, and they gave us good tea from the pure mountain water. Once we tasted the Seventh best water of China. Then mean the seventh of the most sweet and pure water of China. We filled our stomach with it and tried to carry as much as possible home, but a bottle was all

we got. The different views of the mountain were magnificent. We took quite a lot of snapshots.

There was one friend in Kuling whose company father enjoyed a great deal, Haiko, one of the magazine writers. It was on a rainy afternoon he called on us. Father never met him before. He is a kind a person who knows old Chinese very well. He draws Chinese paintings and wears the old Chinese cotton shoes. Since he became familiar with father and mother he came to dine at our home so often and he even went on trips with us. One thing we felt so disappointing on him was that before we left Kuling he promised to give us some squarrels. We didn't know either real ones or artificial ones he made of pine fruits he was going to give us. Well, since he said that sentence, Anor, Meimei, I awaited his coming eagerly, wishing to see in his hands a basket contained of squarrels. Each time he came empty-handed and we comforted ourselves by saying that he was to bring them the next time. Then on our day of departure he came as he said before to see us off. We were on our sedan chairs in front of the travel bureau when he came. There was no squarrel, not even an artificial one. We were really quite angry with him, for we even planned where to keep the squarrels in Shanghai.

Once on our way home from a long trip we passed a porcelain fair. It was on a plain ground, covered up with oil cloth. We stopped and came down and we saw beautiful porcelain on the wooden table of the seller. It was late and the sedan chair carriers hurried us home, so we couldn't buy any. About two days after that we all walked from our home to the fair. Some of them reconized us and said, "Come and buy," to us. The district around Kulaing gives the best porcelain in China and maybe in the world. Each little bowl or spoon was carefully and artisticly painted, and the sufaces are always extremely smooth. There were a lot we liked to buy, but we weren't able to buy all of them of course. We bought a whole set for tea and several decorative vases. One that I like beat is a sky blue vase trimmed on the mouth with a thin dragon of the same color. In buying them we had a lot of fun. The seller always asked for an imeginable price, as if we were foreigners. Mother knew the trick perfectly well and she always said, "Give me 50% discount, or otherwise I won't buy." Then they would say, "It is impossible, we won't sell." Father thought it was inhuman to ask a 50% discount. After about 2 minutes' talking they learned that mother wasn't a greenhorn and then both sides talked price. The thing was then usually sold of at 60 or 70% per cent of the price. It was an art. Sometimes after mother had gone out the fair and they would come out and say, "it is sold", and all walked in again. Sometime after going out again we turned in again and that was the time we yielded.

There wasn't any movie theatre at all in Kuling, and we didn't miss it either, for it seemed there were lots to do in the mountain. The town was really small but rather interesting. There was one big book store where father went often. On the main road the shops were divided into two parts: one more Chinese and the other more for the foreigners. In the Chinese part there were small shops selling old story books and hot pan cakes. We saw them making the cakes we were going to eat. They did it with such skill and experience.

During our stay in Kuling father was doing chapters in "My Country and My people". He typed in the parlor in the morning. We studied also in Kuling. Each morning we practiced our handwriting and read books. Meimei at that time could just draw queer shape figures. While we were studying, she sat there also and drew without being tired.

In the early mornings when we just woke up we played in bed. We used the sheets as an Indian tant and sat inside the tant. Soon mother and father would wake up and we drew the curtains. When we heard father said, "Good morning," immediately we three ran into their room bare-feeted and hopped up into the bed and sat near mother and father. They told us old time stories. Then father sneeked out the house in his pajamas and knocked the windows from outside and said in the American missionaries' Chinese to ask whether Mrs. Lin was at home or not. The American ladies seldom spoke good Chinese for they didn't know how to use the Chinese idioms. Like saying, "Are-you-feeling-fine-or-not-now?" instead of "How do you do?" and they always said a sentence word by word. He imitated very well and we all laughed. Soon we all got up.

The day of departure was quite a sad one. In spite of our delight to go back to the city again, we felt quite sorry to leave this darling little town. That morning we were very excited; after the breakfast we walked down the crooked steps for the last time and arrived at the traveling bureau. We had three sedan chairs as the last time with fruits and bottles of water. Mr. C. saw us off and there we began the journey. In the cooling morning breeze we left Kuling. We turned our heads back a few times to see the fairy valley disappearing behind the tall trees. In some places we could still see a few groups of houses above the clouds.

As we were going down the mountain it became hotter gradually. At last it was breathless when we reached the foot of the mount.

We had to stay in the city Kiukiang for a day before the ship arrived. It was untolerably hot. In the garden hotel, we had a room. It is totally Chinese style, quite nice and is on the bank of the great famous lake. After lunch we lied down on the bed. Each of us was very quiet and later we all got up and sat in the chairs in the garden. There were a lot of potted flowers in the garden. The heat weighed on us a lot especially after the cozy stay in Kuling. From the garden we could still see Kuling mountains with clouds surrounding its waist. We all imagined how people were enjoying the cool air in Kuling.

The night we went to a famous old restaurant. We ordered the famous Kiukiang dishes and enjoyed ourselves tremendously. In the room there was a large fan control by a man. He had several strings in his hand which connected the big fans in each room. So when he pulled the string, the fans fanned and we got breeze. The moon was shining bright that night and we rented a boat that night for it would be impossible to sleep until late in the hotel. There were the boatman and the boatwoman. They rowed very slowly in the middle of the lake. One side there were the bridge arches with the moonlight shining on the winkled water. The other side was the busy side women stooling on the bank and washing and soaping their laundries. It is a funny way of washing; they used a stick to beat the dress. They washed at night because the day was too hot. Far, far in the lake one still heard the beating and chattering on the bank. We sat beside mothers' side and half sleeping half listening to the tales of boatman. It became chilly later but we wouldn't want to go to the hotel yet. Father smoked and talked with the boatman idlely. Mother sat still looking at the water and the neighboring surrounding. Meimei was in mothers arms. So we stayed quietly until eleven and then returned to the hotel.

And then we left for Shanghai.

Tienmushan

By Adet

IN THE year 1935, that summer we went to Tienmushan for a short rest. Tienmushan was about 2 hours drive from Hangchow which was totally a 6-hours trip from Shanghai. Arriving in Hangchow we started with a car to the mountain. The drive was very pretty; we passed rice fields and we went up and down the mountains on the newly-opened roads. In the car with father it is also not tiresome and we always have games or stories or things that amuse everybody.

This vacation was entirely different from the one in Lushan, despite that both were in the mountains. We were going to live in a temple! (Chinese big temples always have rooms for guests and serve meats and all). There wouldn't be many shops or any streets at all. We were really going to be in the mountains.

Through little roads we ascended to the mountain by sedan chairs. It was quiet and shady there. We heard cries of different birds. Meimei asked if there was any tiger there and mother replied she hoped not. It was a full picture of "dark forest" in Meimei's mind. We arrived at the temple where there were only three or four little restaurants in front. The temple was a very big place, with many houses. We were then led to the special house for guests. The house was very clean and neat with the parlor and dining room in the center and 8 best guest rooms divided on the both sides. From the verandah one saw still the thick fog at that time (12 A.M.) and there was the guggling brook right below. We were so glad to find a stream so near for "washing our feet."

We got two big rooms at the back. The furniture was entirely Chinese. We lunched and got settled and that night in bed we were lying tired in the dark and among the murmers of the Brook.

Later we changed to a room which was lighter. Among the guests there, there was only one person which was going to stay for a month or so like us, besides the immediate guests. He was a quite modern young man with heavy eyeglasses just graduated from a certain university. He had always seemed quite unusual in his acts and movements.

The next day we went down to the brook and explored. The water had been quite low lately and it was not deep enough for swimming but nevertheless we went washing feet, including mother.

One night after dinner, when we the children had already retired to the room, our parents were seated outside in the parlor talking to the Mr. Sung. Our door wasn't closed but we had only let down the curtain. Mr. Sung was talking louder and louder and father and mother were listening quietly. I have already forgotten what he was talking but he was very excited then. He had been drinking in the little stores in front of the temple. We peaked behind the curtain and saw his face all red. Mother slipped in and told us he was drunk. We were afraid and remembered that he had a gun. We told mother to come in, but mother whispered that Mr. Sung wanted them to listen and so she went out again. Father didn't want to calm him, for he didn't want to admit that he was drunk. We heard something about fire and light, etc. and we were lying in beds wondering what would happen. We couldn't sleep. Later both father and mother came in after bidding good night to him. We were so glad and we then heard him shouting "turn off the lights! it's dangerous to leave the lights on at night, every light *should* be blew off" and from the window father saw him with his gun and pulling a shivelling monk to blow off the lights. Father didn't tell us that until the next morning. All lights in this house had been blown off for safety and mother and father washed in dark. We heard him shouting along with an electric handlamp in one hand and the frightening gun in the other and followed by that little monk. He was walked through the whole temple like this. It must be dreadful for that monk. He had forced the little monk to blow off the aged "ever-lighted" lamp in the center hall, which might have or have not incurred hours of pardoning to the god from all the monks the next day. Later father heard him went back to his room which was just across the hall from ours and blew off the fire and went to bed himself. Fortunately he didn't fire any gun. The next morning, like a clear morning after storm we met him at lunch. He was a little uneasy about what he did last night, and I think the whole thing was more and bigger than he thought.

The temple was in the waist of the mountain and there was another smaller temple at the top where lived real hermits and meditators. We planned a trip to go up and see some thousand years old trees. Mr. Sung was with us on the trip and with his gun but luckily not with his drunkness. He said there might be tigers in the deep forests, because no one had yet proved that there wasn't. He was in a quite cheerful mood. He let father examine his gun. On the way we passed through several pavillon with names very queer. There then in a damp corner we saw the old trees. They were of pine family, I think and very, very tall. The circumference was not very big, but it took 4 grownup men to surround it. It was foggy and cold and the doubled branches and leaves could not let the sunlight in. We rested for a while—all very quiet and then went on our way up. On one stop where it was very high, mother didn't feel easy at heart. It was because of the heightitude. We hurried and went to the temple. In the temple we had our lunch with Mr. Sung. It was foggy even inside. There were some buddah in the hall and some dogs, and chickens running in the yard. We were having hot lunch. After lunch we sat and drank hot tea. We saw the smoke of the tea left the cups and disappeared into the cold air. Outside the sedan chair carriers were having their lunch and laughing loud. Some thin and enimic monks received us and talked a little. From the window one saw only trees, trees of many kinds and plants of a wet soil and from the yard there were trees and clouds. It was all. Mother and we all wondered how can one live in a place like that. But it was better than the old man who lived entirely alone in a stone hut, fifteen minuits walk from any nearest living residants. We called on him on the way and we entered the stone house. He was rather pleased to see people and talk with them. I think it was every two days that some one from the temple brought him something to eat. He was a monk also; in the hut there were a little golden buddah on the wall and many old books in many bureaus.

We all wondered how was he trained to be able to live all alone in the middle of a forest. We sighed and turned back to the temple.

It was quite pleasant living in that guest house of

the temple. We had hided a maid to do the laundry and cook some extra dishes besides what we had from the temple kitchen. Once we told the maid to buy a chicken for us and the guest-monk came running along telling that it would be better to kill the chicken outside the temple, but it was perfectly all right to cook it in the temple. We did as we were told and the chicken came out all right.

Everyday we went out to the little stream and play. One day we discovered a pool big enough to swim in and we were so glad and we went there both morning and afternoons.

One day father took us all to visit the whole temple, for we hadn't seen half of it yet. There were cheaper rooms for smaller guests, a large room where they meditated with straw cushions in line and each one's name written on it. At the end of the hall there was also a cushion of the same kind but it was seperated by veils on both side, like an other little room. That was where the head-monk meditated.

There was also a big room where they sang the prayers. The room was practically dark though there was a beam of light from the opened door. We all stand by the door and listened. The smoke of incense was quite heavy; all the monks there were kneeling down except those who played the instruments. The prayer was started with a monk singing the scale from the bottom and then the chorus followed; soon the "wooden fish" and the bells and the drums joined in. It was started. The tune turned up and down and the time first got gradually fast and then remained to be fast; once in a while it slowed down and went quick again. Toward the end, the time-keeper "wooden fish" stopped and then the chorus stopped. We had never heard such prayer before and when we returned to our room and we imitated them.

Then we were led to the library or the room of collections. There were many old books all copies by hand. Beside, we saw the essences of real dead buddahism monks. As a rule when a monk is dead, he is to be burned to ashes and if he is a real monk one finds a ball of essence among the ashes. It resembled a pearl and was of the same white color. There were three of them all kept in glass boxes. We were a little bit afraid seeing the thing, but whether they were true essences of the monks or just a bribe for the innocent pilgrims, I don't know.

Besides taking baths and playing in the water, we studied a little bit and played games in the hall.

Once when mother came back from dipping her feet in the stream water, she said she had a stomach ache. We thought it was only of indigestion or a cold, but later the stomach grew painer and mother got a fever. We didn't know what it was. Then mother really got sick, and couldn't get up or eat much. We were worried and a little doctor was called from one of the nearby towns. He came and said it was only indegestion, but the pain didn't cease and the fever was higher. We were in a temple and didn't know what to do and we hoped it would be over soon.

It was awful that at the same time the secretary monk of this temple had just died off. We had seen him in the office outside lying in coach. The feeling was awful and as the custom of the temples the dead man would have three days of singing prayers and knocking wooden-fish for him especially from the other monks in turn and the monks that were singing the prayers were just in the opposite house from the guest house seperated by a courtyard of thirty feet. The whole three days till late at night they were always humming. It was indeed dreadful for mother lying in bed and hearing only the sound of prayers to a dead man. All of us felt awfully and the Mr. Sung was quite nice and came to see mother. I shall add here that the funny act of Mr. Sung was from disappointment in love which he told father later. One night when mother felt really insufferably painful, father had to go to the office and call up the doctor. Generally if we wanted to go to the office we always went out from the side door, walk outside and enter the big gate where the office is, for the road was too crooked and turned a lot inside the temple. That night the little gate was already closed and father *alone* with a electric hand lamp had to pass long corridors, golden buddas in gigantic sizes dark halls to the office and as the lamp casted shadow on the buddas and corridors it had made it worst. Father didn't tell us that he was a little afraid about it till we got to Shanghai. The doctor didn't come and mother was extra nervous stumilated by the humming in the little hall opposite. The three dreadful days were passed finally and we were packed to leave for Shanghai. In the return trip we hired two cars, one for mother and father and the other for us three. Mother was having a fever of F°104 all the way. We left the temple with no regret. It was totally about two weeks that we were there. On the train fortunately it was not crowded in the 1st class and mother could ly down. That evening we arrived home and Dr. Coric was called immediately. It was the kidney trouble from sitting in the cold stream water, (no one would think of it.) and mother was recovered after lying in bed for a month. It's that. It is really what we call in Chinese "going with an eager heart and return with all the fun gone".

But we were so glad that mother got well.

Hangchow

By Adet

It is so hard to talk about Hangchow for we have been there so many times and it is so big and famous and full of places to go. Shall I but then tell one of our trips.

It was in Spring of Easter vacation that we went to Hangchow to see spring there, on the lake and on the hills. Starting off with our own car and chauffeur we were freer about the time. With our suit cases tied to the back of the car and the provisions in the car, we were comfortably seated. Ah-ging opened the gate and all the other servants stood beside the gate and bid us all good-bye while the car drove out. We exclaimed in the car, "Ah—ha, we are off again to Hangchow." The highway to Hangchow was quite newly opened and it was quite a fashionable road also. Every weekend there were always lots of fashionable people going back and forth on this road and in the little news papers there was always a little paragraph about motor car incident on the road. The chauffeur was very careful about driving and if he wasn't he would be reminded to be.

On the road it was quite pleasant. We stopped quite often to get some exercises. Sometimes when the road was not crowded and was away from any town father would drive until we came upon a town where there might be police inquiring about the licences. Father had no license at all. In one part of our journey the road was very near the sea and we could see the fishermen's net. It was where we stopped to have our lunch which we had brought with us. The sea wind blew on us and made us feel that there was still a little bit of winter here. The lunch consisted of roasted chicken and fruits and beverages. It was a sort of picnic in the car. When we had finished, we walked down the pebble beach to see the fishermen. In the large net there were very few fishes including clams and oysters. Far off we could see some ships in the mist. We didn't remain long so we returned to the car and continued our motoring. After lunch we all dozed a bit. Approaching Hangchow there were forests of bamboos on the both sides of the road. Though they were quite thick, but one didn't get the idea of driving in a forest. The bamboos were the sign of approaching Hangchow for us, besides the white letters in blue indicating how many kilomatres to Shanghai and from Hangchow.

After the bamboos there was the suberb of Hangchow and the children on the street shouted as our car passed by. They knew we were strangers in town by looking at the dust on the car and on the wheels.

On the front of West lake was where the "Tiny" Hotel situated. We liked this hotel because the food was good always and the house had got a Chinese touch to it besides all the modern conveniences.

The Yuchuan or "The Brook of Jade" was one of the places where tourists always visited where they were in Hangchow. It was in a temple little bit outside the town. In this temple there was a large pool which contained hundreds of fish, some large as 6 feet and others from one foot up. They were the lucky fish whom the religious Buddahists had brought them to save their lives. They remained in the pool and their families increased. This temple expenses had largely came from there fish-pool ever since it had become a tourist's sight.

Surrounding the pool was a fence and near the fence were the "café seats". We sat in the seats and from the plate of "cakes for fish" we threw the pieces of cakes to the fish and saw them fight for it and devour it. On the table there were tea pots for us and also come Chinese candies and past time melon seeds. There were people everyday even if it rained. In the temple there were peddlers selling old balls of marbles, of jades, of corals and some old pieces of roof from the palace.

These pieces of roof might be real or not, and from these baskets of peddlers one often got precious things for almost nothing. The balls though evidently real ones were sold very cheap also.

In the pool the fish were so crowded together. They often swam to the mouth of the stone wall where the pure water flowed out. They fought for a big piece of cake and often the big ones got it. People seemed to be glad when the big ones got them, because they could swallow up a piece instantly and the small ones had to bite it into small pieces first. Fortunately fishes don't cry, otherwise the "Brook of Jade" won't be so popular.

A monk would always come with a book of contribution and ask the fish-enjoyers whether they would like to do a good deed before God—a contribution of money to the temple. Some Buddahists actually gave out 10 or 20 or 5 dollars, but we being not Buddahists refused but left a dollor or two on the table before we left. Inner from the covered balcony where we were seated, there were many parlors for ladies pilgrims to rest. There were hanged on the wall many writings, both old and new, and many photographs of monks, which were not exactly attractive.

The fishes now might be all killed by the Japanese soldiers who might have cooked them and ate them, despite their Buddahism. But let's hope not.

The famous West lake of Hangchow was really one of most beautiful sceneries. It is beautiful at dawn, in the day, in the evening and at night.

When we arrived that day, we took a boat to see a little that late afternoon. This West lake was divided into two parts; the inner and the outer lakes and they were separated by the two long bridges named after two poets and writers Po Chuy and Su Tungp'o. Besides the two long bridges there were several short bridges and several islands. As I was seated in the boat I could see the general view better than through the willow branches surrounding the lake. Far hills were shown in the not very clear way and the shadows lasted on this mirror-like lake in technicolor. At that hour there were still quite many boats on the lake. These boats were not like the ones in Soochow; they are smaller and less decorated, though very clean. Some were covered with a cloth cover to avoid rain or sun. But generally when it was sunny people left them opened. In several covers of the lake lotus were planted we could see the leaves and the very small buds. It was too early for lotus to appear at that time.

In this dramatic lake there was placed a mornument

in the memory of some governmental affairs. It was like the Eghyptian pole in the Palace de la Concorde in Paris, and imagine such a thing placed on the West lake. The thing was very new and when father saw it, he was so angryed with it. "It spoils the whole view of the West lake," father exclaimed. "Let it be there since it is there," Mother smiled and said.

There was an island where nothing was placed but willow trees and green grass grew on it. Father said, "This is it, isn't it beautiful. I hope the mayor will leave it like this without building up another monument." We saw some scouts doing camping there.

In the West lake there was a peninsula. Many writers, poets, beautiful ladies were buried there. The tombs in Hangchow were a different type from the other. There like half of a ball or rather a bowl turned over on the ground. They were of cement, and very smooth on the surface. A stone piece was placed in front telling on it a brief history of the dead's life or simply his or her name. It was a nice place to be buried in, among the dancing willow tree and the reflection of the lake. There the pilgrims and the travellers passed and admired in Spring and when winter came they could gather in groups and talk.

A famous and melancholy concubine was buried there and many people bowed their heads before them which included father. There was another tomb of a writer who married a stork and sonned a plum tree. He and his wife were buried in the same little garden oppositing each other. Queer man indeed he must have been. This peninsula did not resemble a cemetery at all for there were lots of spaces between one tomb and another.

One more tomb I shall mention. It was a tomb of an intelligent girl named Soo-Little-Little. It was placed in the entrance of one of the short bridges. A pavilion covered her tomb. The pillars of the pavilion were cut on beautiful sentences in admiring her. Sorry am I to say that many peddlers sat on her tomb to get the shade of the pavillion, the peddlers of peaches generally. I wonder how she would feel if she has a spirit some where.

Let's drop the tombs and go back to the scenery. On the bank of this lake there were many many villas of old-time officials. They are real Chinese "big houses" full of luxury. Some of them were opened to public after the owner was broke. These houses were so "deep" as we call it. The little paths turned right and left and sometimes appeared a little house so unexpectly. One knew not how to go out after one was inside and each little place seemed so private and secluded. There was another little museum on the bank of the ancient musical instruments, but it wasn't as interesting as the other villas.

A restaurant named "The house outside the house" facing the lake was the place we would go in Hangchow. Live fishes, shrimps, crabs and clams were kept in a bamboo basket dipped in the lake and when ever one customer asked for a fish they would go to the lake and fetch it. So all things were very fresh there, especially the fishes. Mother once ordered a dish of live shrimps to eat fresh. A dish covered with a bowl was brought to us accompanied by soya-bean sauce and venegar. The live shrimps were covered inside the bowl, so they wouldn't jump all over the table. Mother opened a peak and got a piece of shrimp and immediately recovered the bowl again. Mother said it was good and the rest only took 2 or 3 each. Some escaped and jumped high on the table, but one fell down a dish of sauce and swam in it. Later we took the waiter to fry them and they teasted much better to me at least.

At that time of the year a whole lot of pilgrims came to Hangchow. They were from small towns and they came annually using pilgrimages as a name to see Hangchow.

Some of them walked several hours to get to the destination. Young girls wore pink or purple or blue of the sky dress and old one wore their best silk black dress; each one had a bright yellow sack over his or her shoulder and they contained incenses and books of the temple. The biggest temples in Hangchow were Lingyin and Yowangmiao. Yowangmiao was built in the memory of a faithful general who was assicinated be a traitor. The temple was very rich and the gate and wall were of the rich Chinese red and gold and black. They are colors of dignity. Pilgrims went in and out the gate and the straw cushions in the centre hall was ever occupied by the people kneeling and praying for a good harvest of the year. Goddess of Mercy, I think it was, was the goddess for praying for sons. People kneeled down and put incense on the holders like the catholics put candle in front of their saints. Some popular Buddahs had new coats of gold from their worshippers. The paint shone bright and brillant.

In this Yowangmiao was the tomb of Yo Fei and also were the statues of the traitor and his wife. Two stone statues represented them kneeling down before the faithful general. People now still spitted at the statue after 7 hundred years and the tomb of the respected stood proudly with incense burning in front of them. These pilgrims walked timidly and looked around, but they were enjoying it immensely.

One bright morning we started out to the Mountain of the King of jade. The car drove to the foot of the mountain and the rest of the road we had to go up stone steps. It had really been a curious sight; at each side of the steps about 10 feet apart there was a beggar. These beggars were so ugly, some miam and some blind. They stretched out their hands and sang for pity. Some of them were frightful. One could not imagine a thing like this. It was a gathering of beggars. The reason we found out later was that in this spring time almost every pilgrim with her yellow bag came up to the temple on the top of the mountain, and since they were on pilgrimages they were generally kind-hearted at the moment. They gave pennies to the beggars to show they have done some good deeds. The beggars sometime pretended to be sick and they are often one of the members of the powerful beggar's committee. Father gave us—Anor and I—all together about 40 pennies and let us distribute to any one we liked. Before thirty steps ten pennies were gone and mother said we'd better reserve some, 'cause it was still a long way to go. So we gave one pennies to every 1st person of the 5 on the way, but before we reached the top thirty pennies were gone and I told Anor we had better reserve some for the return trip.

It was a taoist temple and I remember some foreigners taking photographs of the robes and the faces of these Taoist monks. Their faces weren't very particular or anything to me, but I wondered why the foreigners would like to take their pictures. On this hill top there was a very modern terrace overlooking the view around Hangchow.

From there one could see the sea with its tiny leaves of fishing boats, and the opposite side the West lake in full view, with the roofs of villas appearing from the willow trees. We took a cup of tea with some refreshment up there to rest a while before again descending the stairs.

Going down was more easy and faster and we distributed the rest of the pennies while skipping down. The trip as a whole was not as pleasant as the others, but it was a new experience.

On the day before we left Hangchow we went on a picnic trip with some friends. At ten in the morning we started with two cars. The sun was bright and I was so impatient to be caged in the motor car. Passing through the town first and then into the beautiful land scape. The ground grew up slowly apart from the road side into a hill. Every spot we passed by seemed a nice place to get down and stay. After half an hour of driving we came upon to a higher hill with red and purple spots on it. We were excited and when we got near we discovered this was a hillside of cuckoo flowers. Our friends were excited also and we all got down the cars. These flowers were of red, pink, rose color, purple and mixtures of them. To see a hill side of them was very gorgeous. Father described them as young girl of 18, 19 and 20 gorgeous dressed. Indeed they were. We planned to pick them back to Shanghai as they were not planted by any one. But later we thought if we carried them now they would be all dried before we got back, so we decided to pick them on our way back. We didn't even pick one flower. We got into the cars leaving this hill behind.

Finally we came upon a little town with a clear brook running outside it. Mother suggested that we should pic our nics there. All agreed and we moved the baskets to the pebble shore of the bank. The pebbles were clean enough, but the grown up ladies had newspapers on the pebbles first. The food was simple. Several men on wooden pillars tied together passed before us. These wood pillars were to be sent to a certain place. The man tied them with a rope and formed a large board. So it flowed on the water. With a bamboo stick the man could touch the bottom of the brook and push the boat forward. It was light for him because the water was running down in his same direction. The water was very pure and we all washed our hands there afterwards. After the stomaches were satisfied we got up and wandered along the paths and bridges. There were two hills behind us with glorious trees of many kinds. We walked and talked a bit. Later we sent into the cars. Somehow or rather they have decided not to pass the same road. We were disappointed, but mother said, "Tomorrow morning before we start for Shanghai we can come and fetch some."

That afternoon in Hangchow we went to the shops to buy some specialities of the town. Scissors and materials were the principal things. We went to a scissors shop with an emormous scissors hanging outside as a sign and we bought a whole set of scissors of all sizes. These scissors were best for tailorings we always use them instead of foreign scissors. The cloth shop was of Chinese style. It was big and cool inside with a transparent ceiling to give the light. Many sellsmen stood near the cashier and talked. As we came in their conversation was stopped. They came to meet us very attentively. The materials in silk were very good and strong. Mother bought us quite a few pieces.

The night we began to pack and there was a little fish in a glass jar on the table. This fish was caught by father day before after a long waiting. We all had a rod but only father caught a fish—three inches. It was too little to be cooked so father put it proudly in the jar and bossed about it every now and then, but mother only smiled and said, "Yes—3 inches" and then laughed. We three enjoyed the jesting including father. Father replied, "Yes three inches, but it's a fish anyway. Have you caught any fish?"

We could not decide whether it was better to bring it or not.

The next morning surprised we were to find it had jumped out of the jar and it was dead now. Well, it did solve the problem of bring it home or not.

We went out to the lake once more before we had our breakfast. It was misty and cool on the lake. On this road the motor cars and carriages had already waken up the morning but the air of the dawn still remained. A boy came shouting, "hot cake! hot cake!" The cakes looked some fresh in his basket and we bought several pieces. We were surprised to find them so tasty. When we thought of buying more for the trip he was gone already with his basket.

Some how it seemed that we could not have time for the cuckoo flowers. They were to be left in our minds a hill of gorgeous flowers met in surprise outside the city of Hangchow. We started for Shanghai with fish rods without fish and many packages behind the car. The end of a nice and enjoyable vacation. On the way we passed the same villages. On approaching a little town father was driving in the car, and suddenly because of a slip the car went in big zig-zags on the road four or five times. Fortunately the chauffeur was beside him to help father correct. When we got straight we were in front of the sentry guards. They smiled and father smiled back and we went on. Fortunately it wasn't on the high-up road where we might fall into the rice fields. Inside the car we were left and right all about and I was told that I was holding the Tsung-tsi (a kind of Chinese cakes) tight by fear that they might fall on the ground which would not at the least bit harm them. They laughed at me and I did find the whole lot of Tsung-tsi in my arms. That thing had been told as a joke by my two sisters ever since.

The Stories Wang-ma Told Us

By Anor

IN CHINA when my parents were away or when one of us was sick we always told Wangma to tell us stories. Now I can only remember a few.

There was a story which we told Wangma to tell us for many times because it is so interesting. It is Laing the third and Tso. A story of a girl and a boy by the names of Laing and Tso. Laing was the boy and Tso is the girl.

There was a girl named Tso, age sixteen, borned in a rich family. She had two chamber maids. It was spring. One of the maids went and told Tso to go out to the garden once in the whole year to see the green.

So the three went out and just as they were out Tso heard people calling outside for boy students to go to the capital for studies. Tso suddenly got an idea and went quickly into her room and told her maid to go to her father and invite him to Tso's room. And so the father came and asked her what did she want.

"I want to go and study, father" said Tso quite seriously. But her father turned his back and walked to the door, just then Tso called again and told Father her plans:

To dress like a man so that nobody will think that she is a girl; hand a cloth shoe to a bad aunt of hers and if Tso did anything wrong the shoe would get out of shape and the colors faded as a sign.

After a hot arguement Tso finally was to go. So she

started out packing and in a week's time she started her journey. (In older times one had to walk in order to get anywhere—even to another city or state). After three day's walking she finally came to a bridge. There she met a boy. "Where are you going young boy?" The boy named Laing asked Tso. "To the capital my big brother. And you?" Tso replied "The same way my dear brother." "Then let us be brothers and help each other in time of need," Laing replied sincerely. So the two kneeled down and prayed to the earth and the heaven. Thus they started out again the same way. As they talked all the way to the capital Laing did not notice anything as he was a book worm. After a week's time they got to the city. Then in went the two to the school.

"Since we are brothers, now my young one, why don't we be together and sleep in the same bed and same room?" Tso's face got red and didn't know what to do for Laing had already told the school servant to open *one* room.

The night came and Laing said, "Tso brother it is time for bed, why don't you come. Don't stay up so late, I am already half asleep, it is the third candle you are burning now."

Tso: My brother, go to sleep yourself. Don't bother about me. It is always my custom to sleep late. Sleep now.

L. How strange. But at least take off your shoes and be comfortible. (Tso had bound feet and was fraid to let Laing see it).

Tso. My dear brother, when I sleep it is always my way to sleep with shoes.

L. Then come.

Tso jumped in to the bed without changing anything until L. was asleep.

The next morning came and they woke up.

T. Big brother tell me why is it that you kick me so when you are asleep. Now to night we must put a bowl of water in between us and if any one kicks it the next morning he must be punished by the teacher.

(T. didn't sleep the whole night and thought how to keep her feet away from Laing's eyes and from Laing.)

L. Young one, I have never seen such a strange person as you.

T. Ah, that is the sign of good luck!

In the afternoon everybody went swimming with out a thing on.

T. stood on the beach.

L. Tso, why are you not swimming? It certainly is a hot day!

T. Swimming! I can't go into the water, it is too cold.

(Thus Tso went away)

(At the night)

T. Now here is our bowl of water, remember, don't kick it!

L. Ahy, my brother, how strange you are!

At midnight when the water was kicked by Laing, they both woke up because of the wetness. Laing caught sight of the small feet.

T. My big L. How awful! (L didn't answer but stared at Tso's feet, and when she noticed it she immediately covered them with the blankets).

T. Now let us sleep.

L. Tell me, why are your feet so small, like a girls'.

T. That, my brother, is one of the things I can't tell.

Thus they continued their three years at school without any notice. Laing was a book-worm. Three years passed and it was time for Tso to go home. But they after staying together for so long felt for each other. It was time. Tso packed up and began to say good-bye to the teacher who knew she was a girl. Laing insisted on accompanying his "brother" to a certain bridge. So Tso let him.

Tso thought it was time to tell him that his "brother" was a girl. She saw a pair of butterflies flying and said to Laing. "A pair of butterflies flying over the grass, which is male and which is female?" "My brother, don't bother about butterflies," said the book worm answering back. Then when they got to the bridge Tso again asked. "I see a pair of ducks swimming on the river. I ask you to-day which is male and which is female?" "My dear brother, for three years we have been together, why do you choose this sad day of parting to ask me about males and females?" the book-worm answered.

When Tso saw that the book-worm really can't make it out that she was a female she wrote a character which means female backwards on the palm of Laing's and said to Laing, "My brother, I have forgotten what this word is, will you go back and ask the teacher?" Being a real book-worm Laing went back and got forty spanks from the teacher. Meanwhile Tso took out her embroidered pair of girl's shoes and when Laing came back she said, "We can't go across this river with out wading across." So they took off their shoes and wade accross. Tso in purpose left one shoe on the other side of the bank—the girl's shoe—and when they part Tso gave Laing a bracelet and the same pair other in her hand and said to him, "My big brother, when you come back from school, be sure to come to see me, and bring this bracelet with you so that I will know you." So she left. When Laing came back and found the shoe he then knew that Tso was a girl.

When Tso got home she couldn't eat or drink for she was longing for Laing. At the same time Laing had the same. A year passed. Laing came back and saw Tso. Laing proposed to Tso but in a week's time Tso was going to marry Feng.

Laing was so disappointed, he lay in his bed and died. When Tso knew that she was so sad. The wedding day came. Tso was dressed up and seated in a sedan-chair. She told the chair carry to pass through Laing's grave. When they got there Tso jumped out and said "MY brother Laing if you hear me to-day open your grave and let me in."

All of a sudden there came a thunder and the grave opened and Tso jumped in just as the people wanted to pull Tso out the grave closed and all they got was a piece of Tso's dress sticking out the grave. Their parents came and dug out the coffin and found the two just as if asleep and when they thought of carrying them out the grave closed again and a pair of butterflies flew out.

* * * * *

We insisted on hearing some more from Wang ma that day. But she said she had a lot of work to do. We knew that was not true so we pulled her apron to come to a seat and thus she began her story again.

"Well" Wang ma said slowly after a minute's thinking, "this is the story of a feather coat."

There was once a very earnest farmer who thought that he had earned enough money to get married. Just then he found a very beautiful maiden. So they got married. This farmer, since he got a wife, couldn't work at the farm anymore for the maiden was too pretty that he couldn't let his eyes off her. It went on till the couple starved out of hunger the wife said, "My husband, I will draw a picture of myself and let you carry it on your chest. When ever you think of me when you are working just look at the picture and then go to work again as we won't live without working." So the wife did as she said and the man went out to the farm again.

Suddenly there came a big blow of wind and blew the picture away. It happened that that day the king was out for a walk. He saw this picture and picked it up and went to the palace. He commanded the men to get the maiden for him and sent a number of men to search for this girl.

When they got to the farmer's house and found the girl and told them about all the things. So with great difficulties they got the maiden out of the farmer's hut. Before parting the maiden told the farmer secretly that in a certain day she will pretend to be sick and then she will say that she will only eat carrots. (I don't remember exactly what it was), that was sold by a man wearing bird feather coat. And then said the maiden quickly, "You will come with the feather coat and sell me the carrots, etc." Thus the maiden went away.

The king took her for his queen and he lived happily.

The day came when the queen was supposed to be sick. "I feel that I can't eat a thing but carrots sold by a man with feather coat on." So they found her farmer and when the queen saw her husband she told all the ladies and lords to go out and immediately she thrusted the king with a knife, exchange the king's coat and the feather coat and let her husband be the king. When the others had come in the queen said that the carrot seller was a revolutioner and so killed the king.

The Widow and the Bandit

By Anor

WE BEGGED Wangma for another one, but she said that when she began to tell a story we had to hear another one till it was time for bed and so she refused and said she had sewing to do.

We told her that she could sew and at the same time told some stories. When she saw that we left her no peace until she began a story, she went and fatch the sewing box and began another one while putting on her glasses on the lower part of her nose.

* * * * *

There was once a young beautiful woman. She married a count who died a year after. So she stayed alone very sadly. One day a group of bandits came and said to the king. "We must have this woman for a wife if not we will burn the whole city." So the king sent the woman to the palace and told the whole thing to her. The bandits were hiding under a mountain.

The girl told the king to prepare and hide as many armies as possible near the bandit mountain.

The next morning all were ready. The woman went to the top of the mountain without a thing on and when she reached the top she sang so beautifully that all the bandits came out and the minute they came out the king's army came out too and siezed all the bandits. Thus saved the city. The king was so glad and wanted to call the lady to him and reward her. But after the bandits were captured the girl hung herself on a tree and died for she couldn't possibly live again after that morning when she had not a thing on and showed herself to the public.

* * * * *

"Now, be satisfied now, I haven't got time to tell any more as I know you will ask for one more," Wangma said. "But that one was really too short," we answered. "One more and no more." She consented and began again after a while's thinking. This was about a children that was born in a coffin.

It was said that there was a woman who died with a child in her. So they burried her.

In a while the child was bore inside the coffin. The mother changed herself every morning into an ordinary woman and come out to buy some cakes for the baby.

In Szechuen they say that when they give the money for their things they always through the coppers into a basin of water. It happened that the woman used paper money and when she threw the paper money in it didn't sink.

For many a day had this woman done this and the people began to notice. So one day a boy fellowed the woman and when he saw the woman went into the grave and heard the cries of the baby, he was really astonished and went and told the father of this woman about all the things. At last they came and opened the grave. The father found the two alive and so they took the baby out first and when they began to take the woman out the woman fell dead and thus they took the baby home.

The father educated the child and then he became tsuan yuen.

* * * * *

"Now that's finished," Wangma said while trying to get up from the stool. "You promised us one more so come on, one more." We said. We couldn't let her have any peace until she consented to tell us ONE MORE. But at last a low voice called from downstairs for supper. So we went down and missed the story.

The One More Story Wangma Told Us Well It Was About a Snake and a Man.

By Anor

"ONCE upon a time" there was a boy who went to school every day. One day as he went along he saw a little snake on the roadside. So he picked it up and carried it to school. Now that when the teacher was not looking he would open the desk and play with the snake and feed him. Days passed till it was three years that they lived together. One day the teacher found out what was happening and told the child Shu Shein to throw the snake away. So he went to a river and said to the snake "Dear snake, now I have to leave you, but I will see you again."

One day when Shu Shein had grown up and was walking along a road suddenly the rain came and Shu had no place to hide. He saw a house and so went into the house. There was a woman with her maid and they asked him to come. So he did. They treated him very well till the rain stopped and Shu asked for leave but the maidens wouldn't let him. Do you know that the woman was the little snake? But the man didn't know that and took her for an ordinary girl. Later the snake proposed to him. But Shu thought it was a nice place to stay and consented. The next day they got up and had the wedding. He lived there very happily without any doubt. One day the snake told the man to go out to see a show. The husband being so contented went away. But the snake shut up all the doors and windows in the room and stayed in bed, and it was the day that she had to become a snake once a year! She stayed in bed and in a while a snake was in shape and rolled all over the bed. The next day she was well again and Shu did not notice anything.

One day Shu went to a monistary. A monk came out and said, "Hello, but you have got a devil's color on your face, let me look at you?"

So he did and told him that it was because his wife was a snake. The man at first didn't believe it, but the monk couldn't let him go for the monk was a frog and was an enimy with the snake.

So Shu stayed in the monk's house for a long time

and the snake came for she wondered why didn't he come back. The monk when he saw the snake he say a pray in the mouth and a flood came and the snake stayed on a boat and fought with the frog.

At last the snake was changed in to its real form and was locked by the frog in a certain pagoda in Hangchow.

They also had a son who was very wise.

What I Feel About the War

By Anor

I KNOW it is not fit for a child like me to say about what I feel towards the war. But since Father said that I should say something about it I would say it.

There are many horrible stories about the Japs, and how they kill our country men and how they take the Chinese women.

I am glad that we fight on and on without stopping.

But if you reason it there is no reason why Japan should eat us like that bit by bit when we give her already Manchuria. It just makes me sick to hear how they come into China, but the hardest part is that our own Chinese being treators and sell the country in order to live for himself. These treators ought to be hung to death!

Just think of a man selling his own country with money!

There they are, the Japs, almost broke, and yet dare to come into the big China like that.

There is a story of China shaped like a leave and Japan shape like a worm and that's why she comes and eat us like that.

But some one said that China has many big rivers which the worm will not be able to swallow but instead she breaks her teeth so I am sure that there will come an end to this Jap invation.

I say if she fights plainly without bombing the people and killing the children maybe their is a hope of her winning. But like this an undeclared war with all the bombing and sinking other countrie's steamers, they will never think of winning and there is still one country selling gasoline to a country that uses it for killing the women and children!

I feel ashamed of myself when we defeat and if we walk in the park people would whisper to each other "These Chinese." But if we win we would be able to lift the head and walk as others do.

And I hope the war will end soon and a good wind to blow the Japan island down into the sea and there would be no more of the word "Japan".

Some say that it is wrong to hate every Japaneses. But I think one should say it is wrong to kill the poor Chinese. There are those Japanese soldiers whom I think are fathers of children and husbands of wives. Those I think are just as good as the Chinese people. But if they join the army I should say that they and the army are just horrible.

There are some who says

"Leave this problem to God". But if there is a God He will not leave the two fighting like that. After all, each one has to fight her own way out and the wrong is sure to loose.

Please contribute to China, help boycott the Japs. And if we win we will not be looked down as "Chinese waiters and laundry men" again. But as a "STRONG COUNTRY".

Am I Homesick?

By Adet

I HAVE been asked so many times about this question since the time I have been out. The first year the answer was "not yet", the first part of the second year was "sometimes" and the last part of the second year until now was "yes."

At the first year I was all curious about the new world, the new people the new language and the new ways. They seemed to keep me busy enough. China and Chinese were left aside for that while. Soon the new world became familiar, the new people became friends, the new language had gotten used to and the new ways were old by then, and one began to think about China and the old things. Sometimes in a pause the old scenes passed by and brought me to momery. But in New York there was really little time for home sicking. Hurrying to home and to school everyday and in the weekends we were always hurrying for movies or shops or any other things. In buses or elevateds or subways in neither of them I could think for they were going all the time. It had well kept me.

Soon I longed to be in China to be among the same people and same language. As outside in the streets people looked at you as a stranger and made one not at ease. And in other there was this langauge of a foreign tone though I can well understand. That is something between myself and this English language.

I longed to be in China to be able to speak the mother tone to any shop keepers or bus drivers.

Then I remember in the S.M.C. girl schools what a good time I had had. There though the lessons were hard and work was a lot somehow I found time to enjoy myself among the classmates. We had little games in recess time which kept us cheerful for an hour of sitting straight. And I remember when the end of the school came when all the examinations were passed and for the nearly two weeks we went to school just to hear the marks of the examinations and play and wait for the first day of vacation to come. Many of us brought Ping Pong rackets and balls and we played ping pong either kneeling on the floor or on a large table composed of many desks. At most there were two teachers to come into the room everyday. But they had only come to tell us the marks of the examinations or to tell us to be quiet and call the rolls. So we had a good time. Those who wouldn't play any games for the time could read the novels to their pleasure. That was my last few weeks in S.M.C. schools. I always recall these weeks. This is one of the scenes.

The outbreak of the Sino Japanese war was exactly at the end of our first year abroad. The war brought us back a lot and to think of the falls of Soochow, Hangchow and Nanking where we have known pretty well and where we spent many of our vacations and "good times" there. To think that the gracious west lake is no longer enjoyable. No playing boats on the lakes, no pilgrims making the spring time popular. War is war.

Chinese food we longed a lot too. At home we have Chinese food which is very nice and there are Chinese restaurants here too. But many dishes in the Chinese restaurants here we have never teasted before in China. Specialities were what we longed like the Sping rolls of our home town and pepper cakes of the South, which are impossible to get here and also "shredded meat".

One always likes the place better after leaving it. After I have been abroad then I felt many things which were common to me but are precious and beautiful now and I can know better understand how and why are foreigners' impressions on China like that.

Really there isn't any special things which we longed but it is the atmosphere of being in the nation.

Below I shall list some of the things in China which I miss:

—the rickshaw which carries one from a bus station to our home in a rainy day.

—peddlars selling threads and needles and little things like that passing our gate everyday.

—little services for the house maids.

—the little brooks in Kuling where no passer-by could see what we are playing.

—the gatherings on weekends when many of our cousins have returned from school.

—the afternoons in winter to sit around the stove and talk and read and chew melons seeds.

—the picking of flowers on tall trees in front of grand mother's garden.

—the seashore or sea beach where we picked different shell animals.

—the boiling "gathering dish" in winter.

—the roses of our garden.

—the visits to different relatives during the stay in Amoy.

—the fair on April 8 in one of the Shanghai squares. That was in China before, but this time when we return to China things may not be the same.

People Ask Me "Am I Home Sick?"

By Anor

They ask me,
"Anor, are you home sick?"
I answer them
"Oh, yes, I am longing for certain things in China."
They ask me,
"But what things are you longing for?"
I answer them,
"Many things, for rickshaws——
"But why are you longing for rickshaws?"
"Because, rickshaws are wonderful. It's neither to fast nor too slow and in rain we cover it up and the cover has a little window that we could see out."
"And what else do you long for."
"For the Chinese food."
"Why?"
"Because it is delicious, that's all!"
"Why is it delicious?"
"Because they have more flavor and not like the foreign food, you cut a piece of meat during the whole meal."
"And what else?"
"And the language."
"Why?"
"Because we understand each other well and I

feel like a foreigner here for I don't speak English well and in France I don't know how to speak French so it's even worse."

"And what else, Anor?"

"And the people I know, they are nice to me and I like them well."

"And then?"

"And then the house of ours, we have servants at least four or five. We had a lovely garden and lovely house."

"And we don't have it in the West?"*

"Yes, but after all Chinese is Chinese and our admosphere is different."

"So, what more?"

"We had the mountains that we went for summer resort which are not beaches and little brooks and the swimming pools are not built by men but by nature, we picked any place in the brooks that is deeper or deep enough we go swimming. I once did as we came back from a town. They had lovely water along the road. I went and swam there with father and Meimei for nobody could see us. And the lovely brooks. We drank out of them any time when we were thirsty. And the seden chairs. They are so comfortible. And the high mountains. Oh, the air was so clear and with all the Chinese flowers and trees. And there are those strong brown peasants who's teeth are cleaner then any of us without

* *They asked me if there are chairs in China. I said certainly.—Meimei*

using toothpaste and they are so frank and straight. And the poor farmers' children. They are so plump without vitemin A, B, C, or D. They eat only rice and vegetable and a little meat. They were all over the mountain half naked and brown, Oh I enjoy to see that. And the quiet monks. The pale, green, thin monks. How they believe in buddaha make me laugh but how they sing at time, how they go and sit cross legged with two hand closed in front of the chest for contemplation! Oh, I long for China!"

"Oh yeah?" said the American. "And what more?"

"And the Chinese land! China, China, I long for China. My country that is different from the west. All the things in China. The land, the people, the food, the custom! I long for CHINA. If we could go back any time without danger—without war in China—we have decided to go home. How excited I'd be! I remember when we were leaving for America, we had tea at the hotel. I had cocoa, how hot it was. I was excited that I couldn't drink but stooped down on the ground and walked for I was so excited that I didn't know what to do. Mother said that I had to drink that cup of cocoa. So the cocoa burnt my tongue and I swallowed it down with great difficulty. That was the last thing I had. And so we left China behind us!

But now I think my excitement would be greater! How I'd be when my feet step on the China land again. Our own China again and there will be a whole string of people waiting for us.

It will be my great day! We will see the Chinese every where again and will speak smoothly again without hands.

The porters will be Chinese. Every one will be Chinese! Oh, I want to go back!"